Life After Self-Harm

In many countries there has been an alarming increase in rates of suicide and self-harm, yet the stigma attached to these difficulties often leads to sub-optimal care.

Life After Self-Harm: A guide to the future is written for individuals who have deliberately harmed themselves. Developed through a major research project, the contents of the manual have been informed and shaped by many users and expert professionals. Illustrated with multiple case histories, it teaches users important skills:

- for understanding and evaluating self-harm
- for keeping safe in crisis
- for dealing with seemingly insolvable problems
- for developing coping strategies
- for reconnecting with life

Health workers who regularly come into contact with individuals who have self-harmed will find the wealth of practical advice in this book extremely valuable for recommendation to patients either as a self-help book, or in the context of brief therapy.

Ulrike Schmidt is a Consultant Psychiatrist at the Maudsley Hospital and Senior Lecturer at the Institute of Psychiatry, London.

Kate Davidson is a Consultant Clinical Psychologist in Greater Glasgow Primary Care NHS Trust. She is currently Director of the Glasgow Institute of Psychosocial Interventions.

Life After Self-Harm

A guide to the future

Ulrike Schmidt and Kate Davidson

Routledge
Taylor & Francis Group

LONDON AND NEW YORK

First published 2004 by Routledge
27 Church Road, Hove, East Sussex BN3 2FA

Simultaneously published in the USA and Canada
by Routledge
270 Madison Avenue, New York NY 10016

Reprinted 2004 and 2009
27 Church Road, Hove, East Sussex, BN3 2FA
270 Madison Avenue, New York NY 10016

Routledge is an imprint of the Taylor & Francis Group, an Informa business

Typeset in 10/12pt Times by Graphicraft Limited, Hong Kong
Printed and bound in Great Britain by TJ International Ltd, Padstow, Cornwall

This publication has been produced with paper manufactured to strict
environmental standards and with pulp derived from sustainable forests.

British Library Cataloguing in Publication Data
A catalogue record for this book is available from the British Library

Library of Congress Cataloging-in-Publication Data
Schmidt, Ulrike, 1955–
  Life after self-harm : a guide to the future / Ulrike Schmidt and Kate
Davidson.
    p. cm.
  ISBN 1-58391-842-6 (pbk. : alk. paper)
  1. Self-mutilation–Popular works.   2. Self-injurious
behavior–Popular works.   3. Psychotherapy–Popular works.   I. Davidson,
Kate M.   II. Title.
  RC569.5.S45S35 2004
  616.85′82–dc22
                                                        2003016224

ISBN: 978-1-58391-842-5

Contents

Acknowledgements

We would like to acknowledge the support of the POPMACT group in producing this manual. We would also like to acknowledge the grant support from North Thames Region R&D Initiative and the Medical Research Council for the studies using this manual.

Major health warning

People who are suicidal or self-harming are often very vulnerable and need multiple supports: emotional, practical and sometimes through medication. This book is not meant to be a substitute for all these different supports. We are very aware that by making the book available for public consumption we are taking a risk. The risk is that someone who is isolated and still feeling suicidal after an attempt may buy this book as an alternative to seeking help from qualified health professionals. This may be because they feel ashamed about what they have done, or unworthy of any help, or feel that anyone they might approach might be unable to help. This kind of thinking is unfortunately common in people who have self-harmed and may contribute to keeping the person isolated and stuck. So please don't separate yourself from other sources of support.

We originally wrote this book for people who presented to accident and emergency services after attempted suicide or an episode of self-harm. The aim of this was to help people make sense of what had happened, and teach them new, more helpful ways of looking at their situation and of dealing with some of their difficulties. The book was and is intended to be used with the help of another person who can help to guide you through its contents and help you decide which parts of the book might be most relevant for you and which of the skills that the book describes might be most useful to you in your current circumstances.

We want to make it very clear to any potential reader of this book that if you have recently self-harmed and are currently struggling with suicidal thoughts and impulses please do go and seek help. Do go and see your general practitioner, or talk to other health professionals or voluntary organizations that may be able to help. They should be able to help you assess your particular circumstances and needs. Do ask them whether they think it will be safe and useful for you to work with this book and how much additional support they would recommend. Do also show them the book and in particular the note below.

NOTE TO HEALTH CARE PRACTITIONER

You may have been asked by your patient to support their work with this book. The information below will help you decide whether this may be appropriate or not. This book is a self-help manual, based on the principles of cognitive-behavioural therapy. Please do have a look at the introductory paragraphs above, which explain how this book came about, who it is for and how we envisaged it to be used. In our clinical practice we offer the person four to six meetings with a clinician to support their work with the book and to monitor any risks. Clinicians supporting people working with this book need to be trained and competent in the risk assessment and management of people who have self-harmed and who may continue to pose a risk to themselves. It is also highly desirable that any clinician supporting work with the book is familiar with and comfortable with working within a cognitive-behavioural framework. However, it is not necessary for you to be a fully trained cognitive-behavioural therapist.

CHAPTER ONE

Getting started

INTRODUCTION

You have recently attempted to harm yourself. Perhaps it is the first time in your life, perhaps it is something you have done several times before when you felt unable to cope with problems, tensions or crises. Perhaps you wanted to die, perhaps you harmed yourself for a different reason, perhaps you are unsure about why you did what you did.

At the moment you may be experiencing a mixture of feelings and thoughts. You may still feel extremely shaken up by what you did. Part of you may feel pleased or relieved to be alive. You may feel angry that someone stopped you from harming yourself, or you may feel ashamed about what you did. Perhaps you don't want to be reminded of what happened, as the problem or crisis that caused you to harm yourself has now blown over. Perhaps the problem that led you to harm yourself is still looming as large as ever and seems completely impossible to overcome. Perhaps harming yourself is the only way you know of dealing with certain intense feelings or desires and nothing else works as well.

In any case you may be asking yourself why you should bother to read this book. Perhaps you are in two minds about it. You may even be tempted to throw it away and declare it useless before you have looked at it. Feeling that everything is useless is a very common feeling in people who are suicidal. Our intention in writing this book is to get you to stop and think. Don't just say: "I am past being helped, I have tried it all and I know it all."

Our aim is to try to help you to understand why you got to the point at which you harmed yourself and to help you look at whether there might be different ways of dealing with the difficulties that you are facing. We cannot tell you what to do, but you should know that we have tried and tested this book with many different people who have come to see us with similar difficulties to yours. Many of them have found it helpful. So perhaps you should buy yourself some time and read the book. You owe at least that to yourself. What do you have to lose?

YOU ARE NOT ALONE

As health professionals we work with a large number of people who have attempted to harm themselves. Every person is unique, but something that many people who attempt to harm themselves have in common is a **feeling of loneliness and isolation** and that **nobody understands** their particular predicament and how they feel. Another common problem is experiencing **difficulties in relationships** with an important person in your life. In this book you will come across some life stories of people who have harmed themselves. With some of them you may feel you have something in common, with others you may feel you have nothing in common. All the stories are the stories of real people whose names we have changed in order to protect their identity. We hope that their examples can show you that you are not alone.

Calling a spade a spade

You may wonder why in this book we sometimes talk about self-harm and at other times about "attempted suicide". Suicide is the most extreme form of self-harm. Deliberately hurting or harming yourself can mean a lot of other things to you and to other people apart from expressing a desire not to live any more. Because people vary so much in their reasons for hurting themselves and in the degree of their wish to die, we will sometimes talk more generally about self-hurt or self-harm rather than attempted suicide.

WHY DO PEOPLE HARM THEMSELVES?

There are many different reasons why people attempt to harm themselves.

For some people harming themselves is like "pulling an emergency brake on a run-away train". They feel their life has got out of control and they don't quite know how to gain control again or make anyone notice.

Take Sylvia for example.

Sylvia's story

Sylvia is 42 and has a son and a daughter aged 14 and 11. Their father left Sylvia when the children were little and she has had to bring them up single-handedly. Over the last year Sylvia has had lots of trouble with both her children. Both of them have started to truant regularly and Sylvia has had to see their teachers on several occasions. The 14-year-old boy has also got into trouble with the police over vandalizing a telephone booth. On several nights he has stayed out all night. Sometimes he has come home drunk, and Sylvia suspects that he may be taking drugs. Whenever Sylvia has tried to talk to him, he has been uncommunicative or rude. "I was worried sick about him, but he would take no notice of me. We'd have these blazing rows in the middle of the night. I would shout at him and tell him that he'd end up in prison if he wasn't careful and that I'd have to get him put into care – but he wouldn't listen."

At the same time Sylvia's relationship with her boyfriend of three years got worse, as he repeatedly told her she was a bad mother who was unable to keep her boy under control. Sylvia began to feel more and more upset, tense and panicky, thinking that something dreadful was going to happen. She couldn't sleep at night and her GP prescribed some Valium. She also became very irritable: "I would just snap at anybody who crossed me." Sylvia began to drink too much, often on top of the Valium. This led to more arguments with her boyfriend who threatened to leave her. "I was in a total state, I just couldn't cope any more." After one particularly bad argument with her boyfriend one night, Sylvia took an overdose of painkillers and Valium. "All I wanted was for someone to take notice of how rotten I felt. I just wanted all my problems to go away."

For some people harming themselves is **the only way they feel they can reach out to other people, get care or get noticed by others**. People who harm themselves in order to appeal to others may not themselves be fully aware of why they are doing what they are doing. Often they are people who as children did not have the affection, support and care that every child deserves, and may have endured abuse or mental cruelty from their parents and other adults looking after them.

Darren's story

Darren (aged 27) is the oldest of three boys. He has been in prison on several occasions for grievous bodily harm and robbery. His mother was an alcoholic and his parents split up when he was six. Thereafter his mother had a string of boyfriends most of whom had alcohol problems themselves. When Darren was nine his mother's boyfriend sexually abused him and threatened that he'd kill him if he told anyone. Another one of his mother's boyfriends regularly beat her up and, "When one of us boys tried to step in to stop him hurting our mum, he'd get really vicious. Once he smashed my head into the tiled bathroom floor and wouldn't let go. I was so frightened I thought I was going to die." Darren had to go to hospital because of the injuries acquired on that occasion and eventually the children were taken into care: "I can't tell you how many children's homes and foster homes I have been in." At the age of 13 Darren tried to hang himself in his room in the children's home. He was discovered by one of the other boys. "For a while everyone became very concerned about me. I was sent to see a shrink, and one of the workers in the children's home spent a lot of time trying to talk to me. She was the only adult who was ever good to me. However, she stopped working there after a few months." Since then Darren has made over 20 attempts to hurt himself. He has taken overdoses after arguments with his girlfriend. He has cut his wrists after losing a job. "Sometimes I don't know why I do what I do."

Sometimes someone who has previously coped reasonably well with life, gets **overwhelmed by one or several catastrophic events**, which **makes them feel that they are total losers** and that they can't come to terms with. Take William for example:

William's story

William (aged 45) had had his own reasonably successful business. However, during the recession, he lost everything and his wife left him.

"My wife couldn't come to terms with the fact that we had to give up our comfortable life style. She seemed to blame me for the fact that I could no longer provide for her or the children. My teenage children who had been to private schools suddenly found themselves at a rough local comprehensive where my daughter was bullied and teased for her posh accent. My wife then started an affair with an old friend of mine and in the end left. I felt like a complete failure. What was the point of going on? How could I ever recover from the situation?"

William began to think increasingly about not wanting to live any more. At first he pushed those thoughts aside but more and more the idea of committing suicide seemed like his only option. He bought a lot of tablets and waited for a weekend when his daughter was not at home. He then wrote a long letter to his daughter and to his mother apologizing for letting them down. He took the tablets expecting that nobody would want to contact him for several days. However, a friend came to see him and became very suspicious when William didn't come to the door and called for help.

In other cases someone gets **trapped in a situation where they feel increasingly hopeless and can see no way out**. To the outsider the situation may not seem as hopeless but because of the person's particular upbringing, beliefs or values they cannot free themselves from the trap they are in. The story of Sally given below is a case in point.

Sally's story

Sally (aged 24) is the oldest daughter of a Hong Kong Chinese family. She has four younger sisters and brothers. She has grown up in the UK, and has many English friends. "I could never please my father; he wants me to be a good Chinese daughter, but I am not." Sally was the only one of her siblings to stand up against her father. There were daily arguments in the home. "He would shout at me for any reason. He didn't like my hair, my dress, the people I liked, nothing about me. He would always tell me how useless I was, and how I didn't respect him enough. My only way of keeping him quiet for a few days, was to give him some money to feed his gambling habit." Sally felt lonely and unsupported in her family. Her mother never dared to speak out, and her younger brothers openly supported the father. Her sisters like her mother were too frightened to speak out. For a few months Sally moved out from home, however, for financial reasons she moved back home. "I felt like one huge failure. Things got worse at home after I moved back in. My father knew that I had lost my fighting spirit. He began to put increasing pressure on me to get married in the traditional Hong Kong way." Over a bank holiday, Sally had planned to go and visit a friend out of town, but her father forbade her to go. He said he had arranged for her to meet a young man who might be a suitable husband for her. Sally felt trapped. She thought that if she did go to see her friend against her father's will she risked being thrown out from home. However, what she feared most was that in her absence he would take out his anger on her mother and siblings as he had done in the past. She could not see a solution to her difficulties and took a large overdose of painkillers after everyone had gone to bed. Luckily her younger sister, with whom she shared a room, woke up and discovered her.

Sometimes, chronic health problems, especially those that go along with pain and disability make people very hopeless and suicidal, as the example of Ellen shows.

Ellen's story

Ellen is a woman in her forties. She has a good job, lives in a nice part of town, and has no material worries. Suddenly, within a short space of time both of her parents died. "It felt like I was the next one in line." Ellen herself has had problems with arthritis for a number of years, but this suddenly got a lot worse. She was constantly in pain and although she was seen by a number of different specialists, nothing really helped to ease her pain. A referral to the pain clinic seemed like the last resort, and Ellen had pinned a lot of hope on it, yet, nothing much came of it.

Initially, after her parents' death her friends and family rallied around her for support, however, after a while they got fed up with Ellen's irritability and low mood. Ellen felt nobody understood her. One day her niece said to her that she thought Ellen had used up everyone's goodwill and that it was now time for her to pull herself together. "I was so hurt by this, I couldn't stop thinking about her tactless remark. Half of me hadn't wanted to be alive anyway, not in the state I am in, but this was too much. I felt nobody liked me and I was totally useless. I also felt angry with my niece and I thought I am going to show her." Ellen got very drunk that night, and took a lot of tablets. Her niece who was due to visit her that night found her and called an ambulance.

Self-harm through cutting or burning can be a form of self-punishment but it can also be done to **help release tension**, or even to **make the person feel more alive**.

Monica's story

Monica (aged 20) who is black was adopted as a baby by a white family. "In the village where I grew up I was the only black child, I got lots of hassle because of that and always was called names. The teachers did very little to give me support." Although Monica's adoptive parents appeared to be "pillars of society" in the village where she grew up, she actually received very little support and love from them.

"They were always too busy with their million and one good causes, and I think they adopted my brother and me to present this image of the perfect family to the outside world. My adoptive mother was always very critical of me. I was too loud, not pretty enough, not clever enough, too rebellious. I always wanted to know what my real parents were like and I would often day-dream about how I would meet my real mother who would take me away from my adoptive parents."

Throughout her childhood Monica spent most of her summer holidays with her adoptive mother's parents. During her holidays her grandfather regularly sexually abused her. "When I was old enough to realize that what he was doing was wrong, I tried to stay away from him. I told my parents that I wouldn't go to see him anymore. My mother just told me how ungrateful I was after all they had done for me, and that I should be ashamed of myself. In the end I told her what he had done. She was livid. She didn't believe me. She told me that I was a liar and that she should have known better than to adopt me, and that all I had done was to ruin her life." Shortly after, Monica developed an eating disorder; she lost some weight and began to binge and vomit. "I hated myself and my body, I was full of self-disgust." She took large amounts of laxative tablets. "They made me very ill, I had awful stomach cramps and diarrhoea. I felt I deserved the pain." Monica also began to cut herself on a regular basis. "Often I felt so tense and like I was craving for something. I don't know what it was, maybe food, maybe something else. It was an unspeakably awful feeling. Cutting myself helped to deal with it. I did it slowly and meticulously with a razor blade. In a funny sort of way I enjoyed the sharp pain it gave me. I would see my red blood coming out and it would make me feel alive." Monica left home at the age of 18. She began to take drugs and would often get drunk. For a while Monica went through a number of brief relationships with men. "Often when I was drunk I would find myself in bed with someone. On the one hand I needed these one-night stands to make me feel more wanted, on the other hand it would totally increase my self-disgust." Monica then met an older woman and began to have a sexual relationship with her. "For the first time in my life I felt someone loved me. I totally lost myself in this relationship, I only wanted to be with her." However, within a year into the relationship Monica's girlfriend left her very suddenly. "I am nobody now. I am just an empty shell. I don't know who I am or what I am. I sometimes think, perhaps my mother was right, perhaps I did make it all up."

You may have harmed yourself for similar reasons to Sylvia, Darren, William, Sally, Ellen or Monica, or you may have had other reasons for doing so. Everyone is different and has a unique set of circumstances and problems.

TRYING TO UNDERSTAND YOUR REASONS FOR HARMING YOURSELF

Many people find it very difficult to put into words why they harm themselves, because conflicting thoughts and feelings were present at the time, including those that most people don't like owning up to. Perhaps you feel you'd rather forget about what you did. Perhaps at the time you were drunk or had taken some drugs so it is difficult to remember the state of mind that you were in. Perhaps you are the sort of person who very quickly flips from one state of mind to another with little memory for what you felt before.

It is often very helpful to try to remember exactly what happened and to talk to your therapist, health worker or another trusted person about it. The questions below are designed to help jog your memory. Answer the questions, if necessary with the help of your therapist. Do not worry if you do not have the answers to all the questions.

Write down your answers in the spaces given after each question and if necessary continue on a separate sheet of paper.

If you prefer not to write in this book, we have reproduced this and other worksheets at the end of each chapter so that you can either photocopy them or tear them out if you want the contents to be private.

1. What were the specific circumstances that led to you harming yourself?

How did the day start?

When did the thought of harming yourself occur the first time?

Did it grow over a period of time?

Did you battle against it?

2. What were your thoughts and feelings at the time?

Did you feel that your situation was so unbearable that you had to do something and didn't know what else to do?[1]

Did you want to get relief from a terrible state of mind?

Did you want to "blot everything out" or escape for a while from an impossible situation?

Did you feel that you simply lost control of yourself and have no idea why you behaved that way?

Did you want to show how much you love someone?

---

[1] Questions below from Bancroft et al., (1979). (See further reading section at the end of Chapter 6.)

Did you want to make people understand how desperate/hurt or in pain you were feeling?

Did you want to signal to someone that you need help?

Did you want to find out whether someone really loved you?

Did you want to frighten or get your own back on someone or make people sorry for the way they treated you?

Did you want to try to influence a particular person or get them to change their mind?

Did you want to make things easier for others?

Did you want to die?

3. What were your feelings after you harmed yourself?
It is also important to think about how you felt after you had harmed yourself. Did you feel shame? A sense of loss? Did you feel relieved? Write down the feelings you had in the space given below.

Did you feel you had achieved what you had set out to do, perhaps to force another person into a particular course of action or to let someone know how you feel?

4. How did others respond when you harmed yourself?

The reaction of others to what you did can greatly contribute to how you feel.

Tracey's story

Tracey is a 17-year-old student. Her parents have never got on and have recently threatened to split up. When Tracey's boyfriend said he wanted to go out with another girl, she cut her forearms badly: "My mum found me after I had cut my arms. She immediately yelled at me 'You stupid cow. How could you do this to us? As if we didn't have enough problems on our plate.'" Reluctantly the mother took her to the casualty department at the nearest hospital. On the way she kept telling Tracey how useless and selfish she was. At the casualty department the reception was no better. "The person who stitched my cuts was very unfriendly. I felt like dirt."

Think of all the key people in your life – family, friends, relatives. Are there others who know about your attempt? How did they respond to your attempt to harm yourself?

Person   **Their reaction**

1:_____   _____

2:_____   _____

3:_____   _____

4:_____   _____

5:_____   _____

5. How do you feel now?
Try to pause for a moment and think: What have I learnt from going over my attempt and the events and people's responses surrounding it? Has anything caught me by surprise? Have I discovered anything unexpected? Write down your answers to these questions.

It is quite possible that you feel you have got very little out of the exercise or that you feel much the same as before or even worse. You may think: "What good is it doing me to go over all this stuff again and again? It may help other people, but it is certainly not helping me." Try not to rubbish your efforts. Can you remember what it felt like when you first learnt to ride a bicycle, or learnt to swim or drive a car? Did you feel perfectly able to do these things after your first ever attempt at learning them? The answer to this question is likely to be no. What would you say to a young child who during their first ride on a bicycle fell off and bruised their knees and then were very disappointed and upset? Most people would say something like "Well done for making a start. It takes time to learn something new. You will get there in the end." Could you give yourself similar encouragement in the present situation? Write down what you might say to yourself that might be supportive of your efforts.

IS THERE ANYBODY OUT THERE?

Maybe you haven't told any friend or family about your attempt to harm yourself, maybe there are some close others who you would quite like to tell about what has happened, but are not sure whether to do so. Write down below why you haven't told them and what the advantages and disadvantages might be of telling them. In trying to decide whether or not to tell a particular person, think about the following questions: Have you ever told the other person about any of your problems before? How easy was it to talk to this person about other problems that you have had? Did you feel you could trust them? What was their response? Did they listen to you? Did they give you helpful advice? Did you feel better for talking to them? Were they quick to dismiss your difficulties as unimportant? Did they start talking about their own difficulties instead? Were they critical of you, when you tried to discuss difficulties?

Depending on what the answers to these questions are, it may make very good sense not to tell someone about what has happened. There may also be situations where it could be helpful to tell someone else about what has happened.

The people to whom I am close that I haven't told about my attempt(s) to harm myself are:

Person 1:

Person 2:

Person 3:

The reasons for not telling person 1 are:

The good things about telling person 1 about my attempt to harm myself would be:

The not-so-good things about telling person 1 about my attempt to harm myself would be:

The reasons for not telling person 2 are:

The good things about telling person 2 about my attempt to harm myself would be:

The not-so-good things about telling person 2 about my attempt to harm myself would be:

The reasons for not telling person 3 are:

The good things about telling person 3 about my attempt to harm myself would be:

The not-so-good things about telling person 3 about my attempt to harm myself would be:

As a result of doing this exercise you may have decided that there is another person who you trust enough to tell them about your self-harm. Think now about how and when you are going to tell them. It might be useful to take a few moments to imagine yourself in the situation and to write down what you are going to say and then practise saying it aloud.

Alternatively, perhaps the conclusion from this exercise for you is that there really isn't anyone out there for you in your personal life at the moment whom you can trust enough to talk to. Have you thought of approaching your local parish priest, your hostel worker, the Salvation Army or the Samaritans? Don't just say, "There is nobody for me; I might as well give up." Things can and will change if you try.

SOME FURTHER THOUGHTS

It is very easy after you have attempted suicide, to feel very pressurized by others around you (including your therapist!) to give up being suicidal. It is likely that your attempt means a lot of different things to you, positive and negative and that at different times you feel different things about it. So let us try to step back a bit and look at these issues dispassionately. What are the advantages and disadvantages of harming yourself or of committing suicide? You or a member of your family may be shocked and appalled to read that we are trying to get you to think about the positive side of suicide. You may think that we are trying to push you over the edge, or that we are trying to play clever, but very dangerous games with you. This is definitely not the case. If nobody talks with you openly about the advantages of harming yourself or suicide, you may go on in private having these thoughts. It is likely that these will linger and grow stronger and left on your own, you may find it very difficult to recognize the catch or the many catches that these thoughts always have.

The following exercise can be helpful. You may not be ready to do it at this point. It may be better for you to do it later. Discuss with your therapist what would be best. Even though it may be not be right for you to actually apply this exercise at the moment, we still want you to see it.

Exercise

One way of getting a bit clearer in your mind about why you hurt yourself is to draw up a list of advantages and disadvantages of harming yourself. Try to think of what the advantages and disadvantages would be for yourself and for others.

Health warning
Doing this kind of exercise can only work if you do look at both sides. Do NOT do this exercise when you have had alcohol or drugs or are in the frame of mind where you feel like harming yourself. Do it with support from your therapist or another safe person. Do it in a safe environment.

Here is a list of advantages and disadvantages drawn up by Sylvia whom you have heard about above.

Advantages of overdose

- It will show my children how much they are upsetting me.
- My boyfriend will treat me more nicely and not have so many arguments with me.
- It's somehow brought it out into the open that I have hit rock bottom and that has been a great relief.
- Several of my friends have come to see me in hospital feeling very guilty and upset that they didn't notice how bad I felt. They have said that they will stay in touch from now on.
- I can stop struggling for a while.

Disadvantages of overdose

- It doesn't really make any of my problems go away. Where do I go from here?
- My sister called me childish and attention-seeking when she heard what happened.
- My children were very upset. Did I go too far? What if I had really killed myself or done any permanent damage to myself? Who would have looked after them?
- I never really thought I would be capable of doing this kind of thing to myself. How could I lose control like that? I am frightened that it could happen again.

Monica, whom you also met earlier in this chapter, wrote the following list of advantages and disadvantages of cutting herself.

Advantages of cutting	Disadvantages of cutting
Getting people to notice how upset I am	Embarrassment
Getting attention from others	Shame that I haven't been able to cope better
Satisfaction at self-punishment	Worried about people finding out
Calming and relieving	Guilt about upsetting my partner
An escape	What people might think if they see my arms
Leaves a reminder to others and me not to let things get that bad again	
An excuse to cover my arms and legs	
Distraction	

As you can see Monica's list of advantages of continuing to cut was longer than the list of disadvantages. As a next step her therapist got her to rate the importance of each of the advantages and disadvantages listed on a 0 to 10 scale, with 10 being of the greatest importance. This is what Monica came up with:

Advantages of cutting	Disadvantages of cutting
Getting people to notice how upset I am (8)	Embarrassment (6)
Getting attention from others (6)	Shame that I haven't been able to cope better (5)
Satisfaction at self-punishment (5)	Worried about people finding out (4)
Calming and relieving (7)	Guilt about upsetting my partner (4)
An escape (3)	What people might think if they see my arms (4)
Leaves a reminder to others and me not to let things get that bad again (4)	
An excuse to cover my arms and legs (4)	
Distraction (4)	

As you can see the picture becomes even clearer. Monica seems to value the advantages of cutting much more strongly than she is concerned about the disadvantages of cutting.

Next, her therapist asked her to project herself into the future and think of a time 5 to 10 years on from now and to think of what would be the advantages and disadvantages of cutting if she continued with this over all this time. Monica was once again asked to rate the importance of each of her pros and cons on a 0–10 scale. This is what Monica came up with.

Advantages of cutting	Disadvantages of cutting
Some relief (3)	People will be fed up with my cutting and will no longer pay attention to my upset (7)
Self-punishment (4)	My relationship with my partner will have been seriously damaged (6) I won't remember what each scar represents (4) My arms will look horrible and full of scars (9) People will definitely notice and will think I am mad (9)

After this last exercise, Monica was no longer sure that she really wanted to continue with using cutting as a way of dealing with difficult thoughts and feelings.

Below you can fill in your own list of advantages and disadvantages:

Advantages	Disadvantages

Perhaps you find writing this kind of balance sheet too dry and difficult. Another way of thinking about the pros and cons of your hurting yourself is to write two letters. One in which you address your self-hurt as a friend, another in which you address it as an enemy. Here are the letters written by William, whom you met earlier in this chapter and who since his business failed and his wife left him has constantly felt on the brink of suicide.

If you want to do this exercise find the right word to address your self-harm. You can call it whatever you think is best: whether that is dear overdose; dear cutting; dear self-harm; dear cry for help, etc. William very strongly felt he wanted to die when he took the tablets and he decided to write his list of pros and cons using the term suicide rather than self-harm.

Dear Suicide,

> *You are my one and only friend. I am such a terrible failure. Why did this happen to me? Why me? I used to think of myself as quite a shrewd businessman. Where is it all gone? How can I rebuild my life? I do not have the strength to start again. If I end my life at least I won't have to worry about my debts any more.*
>
> *Why did my wife leave me? I go round and round in circles over this. Where did I go wrong? I can't stand the hurt and shame of her leaving me anymore. I hate her for doing this to me. I so want to show her how much she has hurt me.*
>
> *I am such a burden to those few people who have stood by me, my mother and my daughter.*
>
> *Relief would be wonderful. Every night I pray to God to not let me wake up. I go round with a big bottle of sleeping tablets, antidepressants and painkillers in my pockets. I love the soothing rattling noise of the tablets. The thought of you, suicide, gives me strength and comfort, nothing else does.*
>
> *You are the only way out.*
>
> *With love,*
> *William*

William could only write this letter with help from his health worker and found it almost impossible to write a letter that looked at the negative side of suicide.

Suicide, I hate you,

> *I think I hate you so much, because I have been on the receiving end of your brutality. You are so final. You are evil. You don't give people a second chance, you don't allow people to repair things. You are so seductive. I think I have become totally hooked on thinking about you to the exclusion of everything else. You have made me very selfish. My daughter whom I love very much, and my mother who has always believed in me, have tried so hard to support me, and yet I have pushed them away. If I killed myself they would be so upset; maybe my daughter would get over it, as she is still young, but it would break my mum's heart. On second thought, my daughter would probably for the rest of her life blame herself that she hadn't been able to stop me; she has always been a real "daddy's girl". Do I really*

want this cloud to hang over her? If I give in to you, suicide, I will never see my daughter grow up.

I have always thought of myself as a principled person. I have never believed in running away from problems. Suicide is the ultimate cop-out.

Last night I went for a walk in the park. It was almost getting dark. Everything looked beautiful with the spring flowers just coming out. It smelled of freshly cut grass. If I killed myself I would never be able to experience this again.

There must be other people like me out there, people who lose every-thing. Do you try your dirty tricks on all of them? Thanks to you there is nothing I enjoy or want to do any more. I once had lots of things I enjoyed. I am still quite young, I am healthy, I can do things, I can change things if I want. The minute anything comes along now that is difficult or uncomfort-able I think about you. That's what you want, isn't it? But I am not going to let you get away with it. I am going to beat you.

William

If as a result of doing this exercise you suddenly feel much worse, more hopeless and more trapped, or if all the positive reasons for harming yourself or of ending your own life suddenly seem much stronger and more appealing to you, then please do not give in to these urges and read on. Such sudden and major increases in the desire to self-harm are very common in people who have gone down this route before, often with only relatively minor triggers that lead to a sudden lowering in mood.

Please do not give in to these urges and do read on.

WHAT NEXT?

Over the next few chapters we will work with you in trying to help you to look at some of the difficulties that you are facing, give you tools to help you alter the way in which you respond to difficult situations, and handle difficult thoughts and feelings. We all know that changing things can be difficult and will take time. We are not promising you any miracles. There is a lot of hard work ahead of you. Maybe you feel that you are not ready for this. Maybe you still feel too distressed or too angry to do anything. Maybe at the moment everything still seems rather bleak and you may still feel in two minds about harming yourself.

Remember that you have not always felt like this. It is likely that you have coped with problems in the past and that you have had times when you have been glad to be alive. Bad times can and do pass. They do not last forever.

KEY POINTS TO REMEMBER

People who have self-harmed or attempted suicide often feel:

- Lonely and isolated and that nobody understands.
- Overwhelmed by problems, especially relationship difficulties.
- Trapped in a situation where they feel hopeless and can see no way out.
- That they are losers who can't get anything right.

When in this frame of mind it can be very hard to remember that:

- You have not always felt like this.
- Bad times can and do pass. They do not last forever.

WORKSHEET ONE

Understand why you harmed yourself

1. What were the specific circumstances that led to you harming yourself?

How did the day start?

When did the thought of harming yourself occur the first time?

Did it grow over a period of time?

Did you battle against it?

2. What were your thoughts and feelings at the time?

Did you feel that your situation was so unbearable that you had to do something and didn't know what else to do?[2]

---

[2] The questions following are from Bancroft et al., (1979).

Did you want to get relief from a terrible state of mind?

Did you want to "blot everything out" or escape for a while from an impossible situation?

Did you feel that you simply lost control of yourself and have no idea why you behaved that way?

Did you want to show how much you love someone?

Did you want to make people understand how desperate/hurt or in pain you were feeling?

Did you want to signal to someone that you need help?

Did you want to find out whether someone really loved you?

Did you want to frighten or get your own back on someone or make people sorry for the way they treated you?

Did you want to try to influence a particular person or get them to change their mind?

Did you want to make things easier for others?

Did you want to die?

3. What were your feelings after you harmed yourself?

4. How did others respond when you harmed yourself?

Person   **Their reaction**

1:_____   _____

2:_____   _____

3:_____   _____

4:_____   _____

5:_____   _____

5. How do you feel now?

WORKSHEET TWO

Is there anybody out there?

The people to whom I am close that I haven't told about my attempt(s) to harm myself are:

Person 1:

Person 2:

Person 3:

The reasons for not telling person 1 are:

The good things about telling person 1 about my attempt to harm myself would be:

The not-so-good things about telling person 1 about my attempt to harm myself would be:

The reasons for not telling person 2 are:

The good things about telling person 2 about my attempt to harm myself would be:

The not-so-good things about telling person 2 about my attempt to harm myself would be:

The reasons for not telling person 3 are:

The good things about telling person 3 about my attempt to harm myself would be:

The not-so-good things about telling person 3 about my attempt to harm myself would be:

Advantages and disadvantages of self-harm and suicide

Advantages	Disadvantages

CHAPTER TWO

What to do in a crisis

Even if at present you are full of good intentions to work on reconnecting with life, it is very likely that you will come across considerable crises and difficulties and that you may end up feeling suicidal again. The important thing is to be prepared for this and to think now what you can do if such a crisis occurs. Over the course of your therapy and as you work through this book, you should become better at dealing with any crises, but there are a number of things you can do right now to stop yourself from sliding down. In this chapter we will help you develop a written plan for dealing with any crises. This plan should contain important phone numbers of whom to contact when things are getting difficult again, and a number of ways of coping when you notice yourself getting more distressed and suicidal.

GETTING SUPPORT

Is there anybody you can call or visit if you are beginning to feel like harming yourself again? Or even stay with them for a little while? In the first chapter we got you to think about people's responses to your attempt to harm yourself and also close others who you had not told. Is there anybody amongst these people who you could use for support in a crisis, who is likely to listen, and give you time and space? Can you talk to this person now to discuss that you may need their support if in crisis? Write down their name and number on the crisis list below.

KEEPING YOURSELF SAFE

Do you keep stores of tablets at home, for example painkillers, sleeping tablets or antidepressants? Do you keep razor blades, the sharp knife you used to cut yourself, or a noose? Just in case you may feel suicidal again, as a kind of insurance policy? You may say: "Yes, and I am jolly well going to hang on to these things. They make me feel safe." Try to think about it differently. Do you really want to make a life or death decision on the spur of the moment, on impulse at a moment of great distress? Death is forever, whereas distress may only last a while. By getting rid of your tablets and other "weapons" likely to be used to harm yourself you will decrease the risk of any impulsive action.

Drinking large amounts of alcohol will greatly increase the risk of sliding into feeling suicidal again. Don't keep more than a small amount of alcohol at home. If you have a problem with alcohol, Chapter 5 will give you further help.

TRYING NOT TO SLIDE DOWN INTO A PIT OF LONELINESS AND DESPAIR

Below we give you a menu of different coping skills[1] that may be of help in getting the upper hand on your distress. Some of the coping skills described may seem useless or even totally mad to you. Well, not everything works for everybody. The different skills described below are just ideas for you to choose from. There is no right or wrong way of dealing with distress. You may wish to add further strategies not on the list.

DON'T EXPECT MIRACLES! REMEMBER PRACTICE MAKES PERFECT!

Go through the list below carefully. Choose a group of coping skills that seems promising for you, think through whether the skills you have chosen will help you deal with negative feelings, thoughts and suicidal urges, wherever you are and whatever time of day. For example, if your main strategy for coping with distress is to ring a friend or to go out, this may not be terribly helpful if you frequently feel extremely lonely and suicidal at 3:00 a.m. in the morning (unless you have friends who do not mind being called at 3:00 a.m.). Discuss your chosen strategies with your therapist and think them through carefully.

Think also about what you will do if a chosen strategy doesn't work. (It may be that some things work well helping to prevent distress or when you are not yet feeling very low, but that you need to back these up with other strategies for when you feel very distressed and suicidal.) **Write down an exact plan of action and then stick to it.** Add this to your crisis plan, but try to practise your

---

[1] Most of the techniques described, i.e. the distraction skills and self-soothing skills – are taken from or adapted from a book by the American author Dr Marsha Linehan.

skills for coping with distress regularly, even when you are not feeling too down. Monitor carefully how well the techniques you used worked for you.

(1) Distraction skills

This may sound banal, but distracting yourself from distress often works wonders. Things that work best include activities that are physically challenging (sports, digging up the garden, going for a vigorous walk) as these help to remove tension.

Distracting yourself with activities

- Engage in exercise or hobbies.
- Clean the house.
- Go out to a meeting or event.
- Call or visit a friend.
- Play computer games.
- Go for a walk.
- Work.
- Play sports.
- Go out for a meal.
- Have some coffee or tea.
- Chop wood.
- Do gardening.
- Play pinball.
- Have a haircut.

Distract yourself with opposite emotions

Be sure the event creates different and positive emotions. Avoid things that are going to make you more miserable!

- Read emotional books or stories, old letters.
- Watch an emotional movie (scary movies, funny movies, weepy movies).
- Listen to emotional music (funny records, romantic, soul, religious music, marching songs).

Distract yourself with other thoughts

- Count backwards from 10.
- Count colours in a painting or tree, window, anything.
- Play with a jigsaw puzzle, do a crossword.
- Watch TV.
- Read.

Distract yourself with intense sensations

- Squeeze a rubber ball very hard.
- Listen to very loud music.
- Put a rubber band on your wrist, pull out and let go.

(2) Coping with distress through self-soothing

Often when someone feels bad, they forget how important it is to be nice to themselves and look after themselves, especially if others are neglecting them.

- Light a candle and watch the flame.
- Go to your local park and look at the nature around you.
- Listen to beautiful or soothing music, or to invigorating and exciting music.
- Pay attention to the sounds of nature (birds, rainfall, leaves rustling).
- Sing to your favourite songs.
- Call an information number to hear a human voice.
- Take a bubble bath or wash your hair.
- Stroke your cat or dog.
- Soak your feet.
- Put a cold compress on your forehead.
- Sink into a really comfortable chair in your home.
- Ask your flat-mate to bring you coffee in bed or to make you dinner (offer to reciprocate).
- Get a trashy magazine at your corner-shop, go to bed with chocolates and read it.
- Make yourself some toast, curl up in a chair and eat it slowly.
- Take a blanket to the park and sit on it for the afternoon.
- Take a one-hour break from hard work that must be done.

(3) Improve the moment

When people are suicidal they usually have great difficulties conjuring up positive thoughts and memories. It is important to fight actively against letting negative thoughts and memories dominate your mind, as it leads you straight into hopelessness and despair.

- Imagine relaxing scenes, e.g. a beautiful beach with the waves coming in and out.
- Remember a nice time that you have had or a nice place you have been to (say, a holiday, or a relationship) and try to remember every detail of it.
- Imagine everything going well.
- Imagine coping well.

THINGS I STILL WANT TO DO

Write down a list[2] of all the things that you have been meaning to do or complete and have never got round to. Then make a start with doing or completing one of the items on your list. If you had been meaning to visit your aunt Millie in Liverpool for the last three years, make the arrangement now. If you wanted to plant some bulbs in the garden, go out and do it now. Think of small things that you can do at 3:00 a.m. or with little or no money (cleaning the windows, tidying up kitchen cupboards, going to the park to see the roses in bloom, buying a particular book etc.) *and* bigger things, that may need more planning and some money (going on a trip or holiday). Every time you take an item off the list because you have completed it add a new thing. You may worry that if you run out of projects, then the only project left will be to harm yourself. This does not happen. The point of the exercise is to help you reconnect with life and to rekindle your enjoyment and enthusiasm for things again.

Things I have been meaning to do or complete:

1.

2.

3.

4.

5.

6.

7.

Now begin to work on your crisis plan. As therapy progresses you will need to review and update this. It might be useful to transfer your crisis plan onto a small card that you carry around with you wherever you go.

---

[2] Adapted from Ellis and Newman, 1996.

CRISIS PLAN

Crisis numbers:

Therapist's name and number:

GP:

Local hospital accident and emergency department:

Duty psychiatrist:

Samaritans:

Other phone numbers:

If I should begin to feel like hurting myself again I will call one of the following people:

(1)_____

(2)_____

(3)_____

If I can't get through to anyone I will use the following strategies:

(1)

(2)

(3)

(4)

(5)

Your crisis plan may need reviewing and updating on a regular basis. You may also wish to have several copies of it, one to carry around with you, other copies at home left in places where you can easily find it, e.g. near the phone, above your bed or pinned to your fridge.

KEY POINTS TO REMEMBER

- Keep yourself safe by getting rid of tablets and other "weapons" likely to be used to harm yourself.
- Drinking alcohol will greatly increase the risk of feeling suicidal again. Only keep a small amount of alcohol at home.
- Produce a written plan for dealing with crises and keep it with you at all times. Update it regularly.
- Practise your chosen skills for coping with distress on a regular basis. Practice makes perfect.

WORKSHEET FOUR

Things I have been meaning to do or complete

1.

2.

3.

4.

5.

6.

7.

Crisis plan

Crisis numbers:

Therapist's name and number:

GP:

Local hospital accident and emergency department:

Duty psychiatrist:

Samaritans:

Other phone numbers:

If I should begin to feel like hurting myself again I will call one of the following people:

(1)_____

(2)_____

(3)_____

If I can't get through to anyone I will use the following strategies:

(1)

(2)

(3)

(4)

(5)

CHAPTER THREE

Learning to solve problems

HELP! MY LIFE IS A MESS

Most people who are suicidal are faced with multiple problems, some big, some small, some that can't be changed, others that can. What we are often struck by is that the people whom we see who have harmed themselves have lost their fighting spirit, and their ability to think about solutions to their problems. You may be so demoralized, angry or frightened that you feel unable to change anything. Whilst some problems like the death of a loved one, the loss of a relationship, or a chronic or life-threatening illness cannot be reversed, people on the verge of harming themselves often approach *all* their problems as if they were completely unchangeable. Suicide may then seem like the only way out. This is very dangerous thinking. Two American psychologists, Thomas Ellis and Cory Newman, who are experts in helping suicidal people, point out that although it is sometimes said that suicide is the solution to end all problems, in reality suicide is the problem to end all solutions.

Have you seen the film *The Full Monty*? This is a triumph of creative problem solving over hopelessness and suicide. It describes a group of men in Sheffield who all have one thing in common. They have lost their jobs in the steel industry, with little hope of ever getting another one.

One of them has decided there is no point in going on any longer. He is living alone with his elderly mother, who is very ill and about to die. He has no friends and he is stuck in a lonely and boring job as a night watchman in a disused factory. He has lost all hope and cannot see that his life will ever change for the better. He makes a very serious attempt to kill himself by trying to gas himself with the exhaust fumes from his car. Luckily two of the other men manage to rescue him and save his life. At the end of the film, although his mother has died and he has not found a better job, he has made new friends and found a partner and his will to live has returned.

One of the other men, however, played by Robert Carlyle (from the TV series *Hamish Macbeth*), is the true hero of the film. He has been in prison in the past and he has never done well at anything in his life. His problem is that in addition to having lost his job he is involved in a bitter battle over access to his son. His ex-girlfriend is threatening to stop him from seeing the boy as he is in arrears with his maintenance payments. He has to get some money. But how? He comes up with all sorts of crazy and dangerous schemes, including stealing to get some money. The most crazy scheme of all is to stage a "Chippendale"-type male stripper performance with all his friends. At the end of the film, after all sorts of obstacles the group of men do manage to stage one performance, which is quite a success with the local women. Obviously, as they are all perfectly ordinary men they will not be able to go on making a living with stripping, but this doesn't really matter. They have made a bit of money, but much more import-antly, they have become friends and they feel much better about themselves.

Clearly, life is not a movie, but apart from being very funny this film teaches us important lessons. Firstly, you can't predict the future. Things can and do change for the better in people's lives if you have a bit of patience. Secondly, in finding solutions to problems you may sometimes need to look in new and unexpected directions. Thirdly, sometimes it is not so much the solution itself, but what happens on the way to achieving it that may make a difference to how people feel and their future directions in life.

LEARNING TO DISENTANGLE YOUR PROBLEMS

This may sound trivial and you may say "this is rubbish, I know exactly what my problems are". What we often find is that people – especially when they are very distressed – tend to lump several problems into one in their mind. In other words they can only see a great big "avalanche of problems" but not the indi-vidual snowballs that were there first. It can be very helpful to try to disentangle things a bit and to define each problem carefully. Write your problems down in order of their importance in the space provided below. Be as specific and clear as you can so that you can easily tell in the future whether your problem has changed or not. Write for example, "I am sad because I have no friends". Don't just write, "I am unhappy" or "I hate myself".

(1)_____

(2)_____

(3)_____

(4)_____

(5)_____

Now that you have made a list of all the problems that are bothering you at the moment, we will show you how you might deal with some of them. The approach outlined does not work for all problems, but can be helpful for many.

Read through what follows and get your therapist to help you to decide which of your problems you might usefully tackle with the approach outlined below.

STEP 1: FINDING POSSIBLE SOLUTIONS THROUGH BRAINSTORMING

Most people get stuck because in trying to find a solution to a problem they limit themselves in the number of alternative solutions they consider. Often people go round and round in circles between two possible solutions, thinking "Should I or shouldn't I do . . . ?" This can create a lot of tension and upset for the person especially if both potential solutions seem equally attractive or – worse still – equally unattractive. In this kind of situation individuals sometimes resort to harming themselves, simply because they can no longer cope with the tension of being unable to reach a decision.

For most problems there are more than two solutions. The goal of brainstorming is to find as many solutions as you can. Let your imagination run riot. Do not leave anything out just because it seems selfish, crazy, unrealistic, or far-fetched. Do not censor or judge any of the ideas that you come up with. Think of *The Full Monty* here. Jot down anything that comes into your mind. The art is to put all barriers aside, as the following example shows.

Anna's story

Anna (aged 29) had worked for an escort agency for a number of years, when she met Brian, aged 58, a businessman who immediately fell in love with her. "He swept me off my feet. He was so sweet, unlike all the other men I had met before. He showered me with presents. He was so attentive. Within a few weeks of meeting him I moved in with him. I enjoyed our comfortable life style and felt I didn't deserve him." Very soon, however, it turned out that Brian was extremely jealous. He couldn't stand it if Anna ever wanted to go out on her own. He would interrogate her afterwards about where she had been and if he didn't like her answers he would fly into a rage. "He even stopped me seeing my girlfriends. He just wanted me to himself." Afterwards he would say he was sorry and how much he loved her. "I began to feel trapped."

More and more often Anna thought about leaving Brian, but at the same time she was terrified of this option. How would she survive without him? She didn't have a job, she had no skills and she felt that she was getting too old for the escort business. He provided her with company, and a safe and luxurious albeit claustrophobic home. One evening when he was out, Anna got drunk and felt so miserable about the whole situation that she took an overdose.

She completed a brainstorming exercise with the help of her therapist.

- I could leave him for good.
- We could have a trial separation.
- I could move in with my friend Sue for a while.
- I could get pregnant by another man.
- I could commit suicide.
- I could pair Brian off with another woman.
- Every time when I feel I can't leave him I could try to image what he will be like in 15 years and what our life together will be like in 15 years.
- I could marry Brian.
- I could have a child with him.
- I could find a secret lover.
- I could do a computer course.
- I could find a job.
- I could tell him that I will leave him next time he shouts at me.
- I could take all my money and go on a holiday to Barbados and think about what I want to do.
- I could give myself six months during which I won't think about the problem at all.

You may find in looking at your own problems that it is quite difficult to come up with different solutions on your own (at least at first). Is there a friend or family member who could help you with the brainstorming? Alternatively, your therapist will be able to help you to think up new solutions.

STEP 2: LOOKING AT OPTIONS IN DETAIL

Having brainstormed a number of possible solutions, for each option you have found, go through the advantages and disadvantages, even for those solutions that seem silly or outrageous. Again, this might seem like quite a difficult task initially and you may need some help with it.

Below we give you the worked example of a problem identified by Sally the young Chinese woman whom you met in Chapter 1.

The problem – my relationship with my father: he disapproves of my Western ways

Step 1: Finding possible solutions

(a)   Give all my money to my father to pacify him.
(b)   Become the perfect Chinese daughter, give up all my English friends and marry a Chinese man chosen by my father.
(c)   Emigrate to Hong Kong.
(d)   Leave home for good and not tell my family where I've gone.
(e)   Leave home and tell my family where I live.
(f)   Find work elsewhere for a period of time.

Step 2: Looking at options in detail

(a) Give all my money to my father to pacify him

Advantages: He would be pleased as he never seems to have enough money for his gambling.

Disadvantages: I doubt that it would make him feel more positive towards me in the longer term; he already gets more money from me than from any of my siblings. If I ever did want to leave home it would be impossible without any savings.

(b) Become the perfect Chinese daughter, give up all my English friends and marry a Chinese man chosen by my father

Advantages: This would make my father very happy, or so he tells me.

Disadvantages: I would completely have to deny my identity. I like my English friends. I have grown up here. I am half English and half Chinese.

(c) Emigrate to Hong Kong

Advantages: This would make my father happy, although less so than with me being nearby, safely married to someone of his choosing.

Disadvantages: I don't fit in Hong Kong. I've been there several times. I don't like the way of life over there.

(d) Leave home for good and not tell my family where I've gone

Advantages: It would bring a sudden end to all the arguments that have been so wearing.

Disadvantages: I'd feel very lonely and cut off from my mother and sisters specially. I would feel very guilty about my father taking out his anger on my sisters.

(e) Leave home and tell my family where I live

Advantages: This is what I did last time when I left home. My sisters sometimes came to visit me secretly.

Disadvantages: My father might stop me having contact with my sisters and mother. He might become even more vicious towards them if I go and it would all be my fault for leaving them.

(f) Find work elsewhere for a period of time

Advantages: It could give me some time away from home to think things through and reach a decision about what I really want in the long-term.

Disadvantages: It might be difficult to do, my job is pretty specialized and I might not find such a good one elsewhere. My father would be pretty suspicious about my reasons for going away.

STEP 3: CHOOSING A SOLUTION THAT FITS YOU

By going through step 2 you should have a clearer sense of what is right or wrong for you. If you are still unsure what seems to be the best option, there may be several routes to take: You may simply go back to step 1 and create more solutions. But it is possible that even that won't get you any closer to a decision. Perhaps all the solutions you have come up with seem equally tricky or difficult and you may feel a bit like you are caught between the devil and the deep blue sea. Is there one that feels slightly less tricky and difficult than the others? If so, why?

Perhaps despite writing a list of possible solutions and going through all their pros and cons you haven't really connected emotionally with this exercise. Go through all the possible solutions again and try to really imagine in some detail what it would be like to follow certain decision paths. Get your therapist to help you with this, and perhaps even role play different solutions. If all of this still doesn't make you feel any more certain you may not be ready to do anything about the problem you have defined. **STOP HERE! DANGER! DO NOT GO ANY FURTHER!** Do not try to rush things. Do not force yourself to make a decision you can't reach. Can your problem be shelved for a while? What are the pros and cons of doing that? Do you need to sort out some other things first before you consider tackling this big problem that gets you stuck?

Sally, whose case we looked at before quickly discarded option (a) ("Give all my money to my father to pacify him"), option (b) ("Become the perfect Chinese daughter. . . .") and option (c) ("Emigrate to Hong Kong"). She thought she could not carry out option (d) ("Leave home for good and not tell my family where I've gone"), and therefore also discarded it. This left options (e) ("Leave home and tell my family where I live") and (f) ("Find work elsewhere for a period of time"). She had tried option (e) before and it had failed, so repeating it might fail again. After much deliberation she decided that her preferred option was option (f).

Anna, on the other hand, felt completely unable to reach a decision about her relationship with Brian and she decided that for six months she was not going to do anything about trying to solve her relationship difficulty.

STEP 4: FINDING WAYS OF PUTTING YOUR SOLUTION INTO PRACTICE

Think through all the steps needed to reach your solution.

Sally decided that for six months she would have a very close look at different job adverts in the paper. She would also get an updated version of her CV ready and she would talk to her boss, to see whether there might be any jobs coming up in one of the branches of her firm elsewhere. She also decided that she would take an evening course on advanced computer skills to increase her chances of finding a job.

Sally decided that if she hadn't found work elsewhere within six months that she would instead fall back onto option (e).

STEP 5: CARRY OUT YOUR PLAN STEP BY STEP

It may be important to write down exactly **what** you are going to do, **when** you are going to do it by and **how** you are going to do it. This will allow you to check your progress.

Sally, for example wrote down the following:

(1) Go over CV at weekend and re-type it by next Thursday. Then give it to two friends to comment. Have a final version ready in two weeks from now.
(2) Make an appointment with my boss thereafter to discuss my future in the firm.
(3) Buy a newspaper every week for job adverts.

STEP 6: CHECK PROGRESS IN PROBLEM SOLVING

With the help of her plan, Sally was able to check how she was getting on.

After six months, Sally hadn't found a suitable job elsewhere. However, when she had spoken to her boss, he told her how much he valued her work and that with the additional computer qualifications she would be eligible for promotion. With the additional money it was easier for Sally to move out and still continue to make some financial contribution at home (which she did not want to give up).

Sally decided not to move into a flat of her own but instead to share with a friend. Her father predictably was very angry when she moved out and did not want to have any contact with her. After a period of time her sisters and mother began to make contact with her. Living with her friend helped Sally greatly in surviving this difficult period.

ANY QUESTIONS?

As we said above, you may feel that your main problem is too big to be changed or is unchangeable. However, as the result of the one big problem that is clouding your life you may get other problems that you may be able to solve. Often to make a start by sorting out a less important problem can give people a sense of achievement and mastery, which can have a profound effect on reducing feelings of hopelessness. Go back to your list of problems. What is the least frightening of the problems on your problem list? Make a start on that one.

Go through this problem now

My problem is:

Step 1: My possible solutions are:

1.

2.

3.

4.

5.

6.

7.

8.

9.

10.

Further solutions:

Step 2: The advantages and disadvantages of my possible solutions in step 1 are:

1.

Advantages:

Disadvantages:

2.

Advantages:

Disadvantages:

3.

Advantages:

Disadvantages:

4.

Advantages:

Disadvantages:

5.

Advantages:

Disadvantages:

6.

Advantages:

Disadvantages:

7.

Advantages:

Disadvantages:

8.

Advantages:

Disadvantages:

9.

Advantages:

Disadvantages:

10.

Advantages:

Disadvantages:

Step 3: My preferred solution is:

The most important reasons why I want to make these changes are:

Step 4 and Step 5: In order to carry out this solution or make these changes I will need to do the following:

(a)

(b)

(c)

The ways other people can help me are:

(a)

(b)

(c)

I will know that my plan is working if:

Some things that could interfere with my plan are:

I will deal with these difficulties by doing:

Step 6: What progress have I made towards my problems?

You may have found these exercises difficult. The more you practise the better you will get at thinking about problems and at coming up with solutions. Remember, there may not be a perfect solution to your problem. Sometimes problem solving will work very well, at other times less so. Don't just think, "I am hopeless, everything I ever tackle goes wrong. I can never change". We know from clinical research that people who are distressed, depressed or suicidal and who practise problem solving regularly, do end up feeling a lot better in themselves and regain their self-confidence.

KEY POINTS TO REMEMBER

- Many people who self-harm do so because they feel trapped and overwhelmed by their problems and cannot see a way out.
- It is important to try to break out of this trap of hopelessness and despair.
- The skills for solving problems in this chapter can and do work for many people with many different types of problems. You do need to practise these skills regularly to get good at them. Start by working on a small problem you have.
- Applying these skills will make you feel better and regain your self-confidence over time.

WORKSHEET FIVE

Problem list

Write your problems down in order of their importance in the space provided below. Be as specific and clear as you can so that you can easily tell in the future whether your problem has changed or not. Write for example, "I am sad because I have no friends". Don't just write "I am unhappy" or "I hate myself".

(1)_____

(2)_____

(3)_____

(4)_____

(5)_____

(6)_____

Problem solving

My problem is:

Step 1: My possible solutions are:

1.

2.

3.

4.

5.

6.

7.

8.

9.

10.

Further solutions:

Step 2: The advantages and disadvantages of my possible solutions in step 1 are:

1.

Advantages:

Disadvantages:

2.

Advantages:

Disadvantages:

3.

Advantages:

Disadvantages:

4.

Advantages:

Disadvantages:

5.

Advantages:

Disadvantages:

6.

Advantages:

Disadvantages:

7.

Advantages:

Disadvantages:

8.

Advantages:

Disadvantages:

9.

Advantages:

Disadvantages:

10.

Advantages:

Disadvantages:

Step 3: My preferred solution is:

The most important reasons why I want to make these changes are:

Step 4 and Step 5: In order to carry out this solution or make these changes I will need to do the following:

(a)

(b)

(c)

The ways other people can help me are:

(a)

(b)

(c)

I will know that my plan is working if:

Some things that could interfere with my plan are:

I will deal with these difficulties by doing:

Step 6: What progress have I made towards my problems?

CHAPTER FOUR

Learn to change your thinking

Many people who harm themselves often do so to get away from an intolerable or unbearable state of mind.

Mick's story

Mick is a 24-year-old student. He is gay and has had a number of sexual relationships since his mid-teens. At the age of 21 he took an HIV test because he heard that a man with whom he had had a sexual relationship a few years earlier had died of AIDS. "The result of my own HIV test came as a real shock for me. Although I knew it was possible that I could have caught the virus, I didn't really think I had it. Initially, once I knew I felt totally numb. After a few days I began to feel very upset. I would suddenly burst into tears. I went off my food and I couldn't sleep. I was on an emotional roller-coaster for months. The thought that I was HIV-positive was constantly at the back of my mind, spoiling everything. I was very scared of dying, yet I often thought what is the point of going on, this is all too much." Shortly after being diagnosed HIV-positive Mick failed an important exam on his course, as he hadn't been attending lectures or handing his essays in regularly and then his boyfriend suddenly left him for someone else. "I felt completely and utterly rejected and abandoned. It all made perfect sense to me – how could anyone want to have a relationship with me now that I was HIV positive and such a no-hoper in other areas of my life too. There seemed to be nobody and nothing out there for me, things could only get worse. My boyfriend and I had had a huge row on the night he told me he was going to leave me and after he was gone I went through the bathroom cabinet and took all the tablets I could find . . . Luckily, my flat-mate then arrived and she called an ambulance and got me to hospital.

Our thoughts, moods, physical reactions and the way we behave in response to certain situations all influence each other.

In Mick's case one prominent theme in his thinking was that now that he was HIV-positive, people wouldn't want to be with him, that he was different and that people might think he was disgusting. These thoughts made him very depressed and he stopped smiling at people and stopped calling friends. This led to a marked change in how others responded to him. Apart from one very good friend, other friends and acquaintances called him much less often. He took this as confirmation that he was unlikable. Even with his best friend he started behaving differently as he thought "James is only calling me out of pity". Luckily, James knew Mick well enough to convince him that this was not true. Mick also stopped attending lectures and tutorials for his course and got behind on his coursework, leading to him failing an exam, and contributing to his negative view of himself.

Another theme in Mick's thoughts was worrying about getting ill. He would often wake up in the middle of the night thinking about his illness and how it might progress. He would get increasingly anxious. He would often notice his heart beating very fast and then would break out in a cold sweat and wonder whether this was the first sign of him getting physically ill. This would lead to a cascade of further health worries and mounting anxiety till he felt totally panic-stricken.

People like Mick, desperate enough to hurt themselves, often are terribly confused about what they are feeling and thinking and just experience their situation as unbearable and feel that they are losing control. They think that they are trapped with no way out.

A starting point in regaining control and in feeling less overwhelmed by intense negative moods and thoughts is to try to write down what you are feeling and thinking in certain situations and to notice the links between the two. This is more easily said than done and requires a bit of practice. The following series of exercises are designed to help you to become more aware of what you are feeling and thinking and to break up the task into more manageable steps.

LET'S MAKE A START BY LOOKING AT MOODS

Strong moods are usually a sign that something important is going on. Some people find it easy to be aware of their thoughts and mood. They can describe what they are feeling and thinking whilst others find it almost impossible. Some moods are more difficult to own up to than others, for example shame, anger or jealousy. In describing your moods you may feel tempted to say "I felt terrible all week". Try to be more specific, both in describing *what* you feel but also in describing the *situation* in which a particular mood occurred. On the whole it is best to think about quite a brief time frame (something like half an hour) in describing a situation. This is important, as the purpose of looking at your different moods in different situations is to build up a picture of what triggers certain moods and thoughts.

Below is a list of moods to help you describe the range of different moods you may experience at times. The list is not meant to be comprehensive and you may wish to add other moods important for you:

angry

anxious

appalled

apprehensive

ashamed

bitter

contemptible

contemptuous

disappointed

disgusted

ecstatic

embarrassed

empty

excited

exposed

envious

frustrated

guilty

humiliated

irritated

jealous

joyful

happy

loving

needy

nervous

outraged

over-the-moon

panic-stricken

peaceful

sad

sneery

self-conscious

tense

terrified

triumphant

worried

What are your predominant moods *right now*? Choose one or several of the words from the list or add your own.

1.

2.

3.

Now describe the strength of these moods on a scale of 0% to 100% (where 0% is the absence of a certain mood and 100% is the strongest intensity imaginable of a certain mood).

Mood 1: Intensity ____

Mood 2: Intensity ____

Mood 3: Intensity ____

As we said above it can at times be quite difficult to identify and describe your moods. Maybe at present you don't feel much at all. So let's look at what happened yesterday. Identify at least three different situations and moods.

Situation	Moods (describe in one word what you felt; rate intensity %)
1.	
2.	

Situation	Moods (describe in one word what you felt; rate intensity %)
3.	

LINKING FEELINGS AND THOUGHTS

Whenever we experience a mood there are usually thoughts accompanying it. It is sometimes difficult to know what comes first in a certain situation, the thought or the mood, especially if things happen very fast. People usually are more aware of their moods than of their thoughts, but quite often it is the thoughts or how we interpret a situation that trigger the moods we then experience.

For example, shortly after he was diagnosed, Mick told his tutor at university about his HIV status. He told him in confidence, but afterwards was quite worried about whether the tutor would keep to his promise. A few days later Mick happened to pass another member of staff in the corridor. This person who was usually very friendly to students suddenly ignored Mick. Mick's first thoughts were, "He knows and he doesn't like me any more. He can't even be bothered to look at me or say hello." Mick's immediate response was to feel very upset and tearful.

Once a person is in a state of mind where they are distressed, angry or upset their thinking often becomes less balanced and more prone to distortions than usual. This then usually feeds into their negative mood and makes it worse. Distressing, difficult, or negative moods may often lead to behaviour with distressing, difficult or negative consequences.

In his upset and tearful state, the first thoughts that came to Mick's mind were about his tutor. He thought, "The bastard, how dare he betray my request for confidentiality. I am going to show him . . ." Mick's immediate impulse at this point was to want to storm into his tutor's office and confront him, thinking that his tutor must have betrayed his request for confidentiality.

Try to put yourself into Mick's shoes. Could there be any alternative explanations for why the member of staff did not say hello to Mick when he met him?

Two possible outcomes

Let's stay with Mick and think about what could possibly happen next.

Outcome 1

With all these thoughts and feelings going round and round in his mind, Mick bumped into his friend James. James immediately recognized that Mick wasn't feeling very well. He asked him what was the matter and Mick told him over a cup of coffee in the college cafeteria. James, who knew both the member of staff that Mick bumped into and Mick's tutor, tried to get Mick to see that his tutor is usually someone who behaves very professionally and would be very unlikely to betray Mick's confidence.

He also got Mick to think about the possibility that the member of staff may have had reasons of his own for not saying hello to Mick. Maybe he was deeply in thought, maybe he didn't recognize Mick, perhaps he had forgotten his glasses, or perhaps something upsetting had happened to him like an argument with his wife or a car crash. James also said to Mick that perhaps there might be some people who would be put off by him being HIV-positive and who might treat him unfairly because of this, but that these were ignorant people and why should Mick suffer because of them? After his conversation with James, Mick felt much better. When he had his next meeting with his tutor, his tutor spontaneously said that he had been quite worried about Mick at their previous meeting as Mick didn't seem to believe him that he would keep the knowledge of Mick's HIV status safe.

Outcome 2

Mick stormed to his tutor's office, but his tutor wasn't there. His secretary said that he was in an important meeting and not to be disturbed. In his distraught state Mick thought that his tutor was deliberately avoiding him. He took this as further proof of the tutor's betrayal and of how people didn't like him any more and how lonely and isolated he was. Instead of going to his next class Mick went home and got drunk. Sinking into deeper and deeper despair he decided that he might as well kill himself and took an overdose.

Unfortunately, in real life there often isn't someone like James around who appears at the right moment to rescue us when our thoughts and feelings are running riot. It is therefore important to learn some of the reasoning skills that James used with Mick yourself, so that instead of relying on having a friend there you can rescue yourself from overwhelming thoughts and feelings.

But before you learn to reason with yourself you must learn to identify your thoughts. Remember that strong emotions usually lead to distorted thinking and thinking in this way leads to more extreme and unpleasant emotions.

A THOUGHT IS NOT A FACT: LEARN TO RECOGNIZE SKEWED THINKING

Just because a friend of yours is convinced that England will win the Football World Cup next time round, this won't necessarily happen. Actually, there is only a slim chance that it will happen. You may think that this is pretty obvious, but when it comes to thoughts like, "I am totally worthless", "nobody likes me", "I can't trust anybody", "my life has always been miserable and lonely, there is no future for me", or "I can't live without my husband, I might as well be dead" you may be much more ready to accept these thoughts as facts. Yet if your best friend kept saying things like these about themselves, their life or their future, you would have no problem recognizing that although they aren't feeling good at the moment, of course they are not worthless. You would be able to help them remember that their life had not always been miserable and lonely, and that you can think of plenty of good times that the two of you had together. So the real difficulty is to detect this skewed kind of thinking when it concerns yourself.

Below we have listed a number of typical ways in which people's thinking can be skewed or biased (adapted from Blackburn, 1994).

Jumping to conclusions

This can take two forms: In *mind-reading* you assume that other people are thinking bad things about you, but you have no valid evidence for this. For example: "My friends and family have given up on me, I am just a burden to everyone." Even though friends and families may sometimes be fed up or even angry with someone who is distressed it doesn't mean they are totally fed up and will remain so forever.

In *fortune-telling* you make negative predictions about the future without really knowing what the future holds. "Nobody will miss me if I die." Suicidal people usually totally underestimate the effect their self-harm or death has on those around them.

Black-and-white thinking or all-or-nothing thinking

Thought: "If I don't please others at all times I am selfish and unlovable" or "If I am not perfect, I am a total failure". Most people aren't all good or all bad, they are a bit of both.

Are you expecting yourself to be perfect? You can't get everything right all the time. It is just not possible. Are you setting impossibly high standards for yourself and then telling yourself off for making mistakes, or behaving in ways you would rather not have done? Accepting that you can't be perfect does not mean you have to give up trying to do things well. Instead of getting upset, when you get things wrong or don't do them as well as you had hoped for, you can learn from your errors and difficulties.

Are you expecting more of yourself than you would of someone else? If another person was in your situation what would you think about them? Would you be as tough on them as yourself? Throw out your double standards and try to be as kind to yourself as you would be to others. It won't mean you'll end up in chaos or collapse.

Overgeneralization

Thought: "I will never be happy" or "I will never be able to find a partner".

Overgeneralization is seeing a single negative event as a never-ending cycle of defeat. Watch out for global words in your thinking, words like always/never, everyone/no-one, everything/nothing. Most situations are much less clear-cut than that. Usually it's sometimes, some people and some things.

Labelling (e.g. "I am an idiot"; "I am despicable") is an extreme form of overgeneralization. Instead of describing specifically what error or mistake you made you attach a negative label to yourself.

Personalization

Example: "I only have myself to blame for the fact that my marriage failed."

Are you blaming yourself for something that is not really your fault? Many people who have harmed themselves blame themselves for being in a crisis, or for not coping, or for being distressed. They criticize themselves for being weak-willed. Blaming yourself for your difficulties will only make you more miserable and isn't helpful.

Mental filter

Example: "Nothing good ever happens to me."

This is dwelling on the negative and filtering out the positive. When people are in a state of crisis, they often overlook problems they handled successfully in the past and resources that would help them to overcome current difficulties.

Are you paying attention only to the negative side of things? For example, are you dwelling on all the things that have gone wrong in your life and overlooking or disregarding things you have enjoyed or done well? E.g. "It was nothing special I did, when I stood up to my boss, anyone could have done that."

Catastrophizing

"My life is terrible, I can't stand it any more. Things can only get worse."

Are you overestimating the chances of disaster, death and destruction? Or are you exaggerating the importance of something that has happened? (E.g. "Failing this exam was the most awful thing that could have happened to me.") What difference does a particular event really make to your life? What will you think about it in 6 weeks, 6 months or in a few years? Do you think you will you even remember it? Will anyone else?

Asking unanswerable questions

Example: "Why am I so useless? Why do other people always get a better deal than me? Why is everything so difficult?" Dwelling on questions like these will definitely feed your distress. Stop whipping yourself.

Do you recognize some of your own ways of thinking in the examples given above? Do not worry, if you can't fit your own thoughts neatly into the categories above, as they are overlapping. The main point is that all these skewed ways of thinking will trip you up and push you into believing that there is nothing you can do to change your situation. Pessimism about the chance of changing things makes you give up before you even started. You can't know that there is no solution to your problems until you try.

WHERE DOES THIS KIND OF SKEWED THINKING COME FROM?

There is not a simple answer to this question. We do know that people differ tremendously in their ways of feeling and thinking about different situations. Some people are more prone to certain thoughts and moods than others. Our life experiences powerfully influence the beliefs (and moods) that colour our lives. If a person grew up in an environment where they could not trust any of the adults who looked after them, because they were unpredictable or uninterested or because they abused the child sexually, physically or emotionally, the person may grow up with fundamental mistrust in anybody and anything and feeling extremely bad about themselves, too. They will be prone to low mood that in turn will lead to negative and hopeless thoughts.

Mick came from a large family and had always been made to feel the odd one out. As a child Mick had been bullied by his older brothers and other boys. They called him a "swot". Mick was the only one from his family to go to university and his parents were very critical about this, comparing him to his brothers who had left school early to earn good money. He was made to feel that he wasn't quite right from very early on in his family because he didn't share his father's and brothers' interests and this was further reinforced once he told his family that he was gay. His father couldn't cope with this at all and the rest of the family treated it as an embarrassing secret. So it is not surprising that with the sudden and severe stress of being diagnosed as HIV-positive he should have strong thoughts about being unacceptable to people and a failure all-round. These thoughts were further reinforced by his partner's sudden decision to leave him and failing his exam.

Habitual ways of thinking tend to happen quite automatically before we have had a chance to really assess the situation. Because they are so familiar, we tend to accept our automatic thoughts as correct, as if they are facts and we do not think of questioning them. This is even more so if the thoughts lead to strong emotions such as shame or guilt that, in themselves, cause us to think in a more extreme way. Sometimes habitual ways of thinking are harmless or even helpful, but when they produce unpleasant results, we need to look at them more carefully.

Remember that we have all *learnt* to think the way that we do and if we have learnt to think automatically in unhelpful ways, we *can* learn to think differently.

THE MEMORY TRAP OR WHY DOES MY THINKING OVERWHELM ME?

At the point of being suicidal a person will often be very negative about their current life circumstances, but in addition all their memories, too, are extremely negative. Based on this they may reach the conclusion that their only way out is suicide.

In his excellent book *The Cry of Pain* Professor Mark Williams talks about the "memory trap" that suicidal people fall into. He notes:

> "the importance of memory is hard to overstate. Memory provides us with all our knowledge about who we are, what we have been through in the past: happy times and sad times. It is on the basis of our memory that we make predictions about the future. If our memory is biased or faulty, then our predictions are also likely to be biased or faulty. Our self-esteem also depends on memory. Self-esteem is based upon our past successes and failures, and how successfully we have navigated a path through the world so far."

He describes research carried out by him and others, which shows that people who are depressed or suicidal are much faster at remembering negative rather than positive things that happened to them. They also find it much more difficult than other people to remember specific events, so rather than remembering a particular occasion when someone hurt them they might remember "People always hurt me". Because of this memory trap it is easy for a person to get locked into a cycle of increasing despair, hopelessness and ultimately suicidality from which it is difficult to escape. Being aware of this memory trap is the first step in battling against it. The techniques later on in this chapter and also some of the techniques in Chapter 2 (e.g. try to remember a nice time or nice place with all the details) will help in beating the memory trap and skewed automatic thinking.

STARTING A THOUGHT RECORD

Try to think back over the situations and moods that you described in the exercise above and try to remember what your thoughts were immediately before you started feeling a certain way. Put your thoughts down in the thought record below and see whether you can identify any skewed thinking. This may be difficult at first. Ask your therapist to help you.

Situation	Moods	Thoughts (Pay particular attention to what was going through your mind just before you started to feel this way)

It is likely that a number of different thoughts will have come to your mind, some more and some less important as shown in the following example.

Jane's story

Jane came from a very religious family. Her parents and two sisters considered sex before marriage as sinful and contraception was never discussed in the family. When Jane had her first boyfriend there were tirades of criticism from her mother who felt that Jane shouldn't go out with him or indeed anybody. At age 19, Jane got pregnant in a casual relationship with a man who pushed her into having sex when they both were quite drunk. Jane decided to have a termination of pregnancy but afterwards was frequently plagued by thoughts about being a bad, unlovable person. At 28, Jane had been left by her boyfriend of five years. He had suddenly gone off with another woman and only after he had left, Jane learnt that several of their mutual friends had long known that he was having an affair. Understandably, Jane felt very betrayed. After a drunken argument one night when her ex-boyfriend had come to her flat to pick up some of his belongings she took an overdose.

For a long time thereafter Jane found it very difficult to consider having another relationship. She avoided going out and if she was introduced to a man who seemed likable she totally clammed up.

Jane's thought record

Jane's friend Claire, who knew what was happening to her, decided that Jane had hibernated for long enough and invited Jane for dinner together with her brother Mark, whom Jane had never met. We asked Jane to keep a record of her thoughts of her encounter with Mark.

Situation	Moods	Automatic thoughts
Friday, 8:00 p.m. Going to dinner with my friend Claire, Claire's boyfriend and Claire's brother Mark.		
Being introduced to Mark, who seems really nice.	Tense 90% Anxious 90% Curious 50%	I look awful. **(Personalization)**
Mark talking to me at length during the dinner.	Feeling judged 90%	Mark will sense that there is something funny about me that seems to give off the wrong signal. **(Personalization)** I am boring. I have nothing to say. **(Labelling)** Mark knows about my previous boyfriend leaving me and he is probably only talking to me out of pity. **(Mind-reading, jumping to conclusions)** I will never find another partner again. **(Overgeneralization)**

You can see from Jane's thought record that there is only a small step from the kind of unhelpful and skewed thoughts she has had to the slippery slope of feeling very hopeless and helpless and her beginning to think suicidal thoughts again.

HOW TO CHALLENGE BIASED THINKING

Here are some general tips and hints for you so you can start your own thought record. In trying to challenge your most distressing automatic thoughts (hot thoughts) you can use different strategies:

(1) Ask yourself "What is the evidence for this thought?"

Try to consider your hot thoughts as guesses, something that you keep an open mind about. Gathering evidence that doesn't support your hot thoughts can help you to think more clearly about your situation and may help reduce distressing moods.

We asked Jane to circle which of these thoughts was the one that was most upsetting and most strongly emotionally charged for her. She circled "I am boring. I have nothing to say", which was the thought most closely linked to her strong feeling of tension and anxiety and feeling judged. As we know, strong moods tend to make it difficult for us to be aware of all aspects of a particular situation – they tend to produce "tunnel-vision" so that we can only see one possibility, whereas in reality, there are many.

We then asked Jane to write down any evidence she had that would support her most distressing thoughts and any evidence she had that would suggest that her "hot thoughts" weren't completely true all the time. In a further step we asked her to write down some more balanced alternative thoughts – see opposite for what emerged.

When Jane had done this exercise she still felt rather nervous about her encounter with Mark, but she could now rate the mood as less strong.

Taking a broader view is difficult at first, and takes practice, but the more you practise, the easier it becomes.

(2) Another way of dealing with difficult thoughts is to ask yourself "How else can I view this?"

The following questions can help you to regain your cool and a different perspective on what is happening:

How would you have looked at this situation before your present difficulties started?

How will you look on it in five years' time?

How would a good friend of yours look at it?

Situation	Moods	Distressing thoughts	Evidence that supports the hot thought	Evidence that does not support the hot thought	Alternative/balanced thought
Friday, 8:00 p.m. Dinner with my friend Claire, her boyfriend and her brother Mark.					
Being introduced to Mark, who seems really nice.	Tense 90% Anxious 90% Curious 50% Feeling judged 90%	I look awful. (Personalization)	Since the break up of my relationship I have not looked my best.	Yesterday a customer at work said I had beautiful hair.	Even if I don't look my best, that doesn't mean there is nothing attractive about me.
Mark talking to me at length during the dinner.		I am boring. I have nothing to say. (Labelling)	I said very little when he talked to me about his work.	I did have a lot to say when we talked about films.	Often people quite like it when you listen; Mark didn't seem to mind me being quiet at times.
		Mark knows about my boyfriend leaving me and he is probably only talking to me out of pity. (Mind-reading, jumping to conclusions)	Claire and her brother are very close. It is likely that she will have said something to him.	He talked to me for quite a long time and seemed involved in the conversation.	He did seem to like me a bit, so what if he also felt a bit sorry for me?
		I will never find another partner again. (Overgeneralization)	I have not found a new partner since my relationship broke up 6 months ago.	I have in the past found it quite easy to meet new partners.	I have been badly affected by the break up and I have needed time to get over it. That doesn't mean I will never date anyone again.

How would you look at it if a good friend described this situation to you?

(3) A third strategy is to simply ask yourself "Where is this kind of thinking getting me?"

Go back to the example of Jane. What if she had totally given in to her thoughts that she was unattractive, boring, and would never find another partner? This would probably stop her completely from going out, becoming more miserable, lonely, isolated, feeling more negative about herself and making it less likely that she would find a partner.

Some words of warning

You may want to write this chapter off as too difficult, because writing down your thoughts and feelings may seem a bit weird or artificial to you. Writing is a skill, like any other skill, which needs practice. You will need to write a thought record of approximately 20 to 30 difficult situations to become fluent at it and for it to make a difference. So don't give up prematurely, give yourself a chance. Get your therapist to help you if you get stuck.

KEY POINTS TO REMEMBER

In this chapter you should have learnt to:

• Name and rate the intensity of different moods.
• Recognize and rate the intensity of different types of skewed and unhelpful ways of thinking.
• Keep a thought record that helps you challenge skewed and unhelpful ways of thinking.
• Above all: Remember a thought is not a fact.

Looking at moods

What are your predominant moods *right now*? Choose one or several of the words from the list or add your own.

1.

2.

3.

Now describe the strength of these moods on a scale of 0% to 100% (where 0% is the absence of a certain mood and 100% is the strongest intensity imaginable of a certain mood).

Mood 1: Intensity ____

Mood 2: Intensity ____

Mood 3: Intensity ____

Identify at least three different situations and moods.

Situation	Moods (describe in one word what you felt; rate intensity %)
1.	
2.	
3.	

Starting a thought record

Situation	Moods	Thoughts (Pay particular attention to what was going through your mind just before you started to feel this way)

Thought record

Situation	Moods	Automatic thoughts	Evidence in support of the hot thought	Evidence that does not support the hot thought	Alternative balanced thought	Rate mood now

CHAPTER FIVE

Alcohol, drugs and pills:
do you need to cut down or stop?

People in crisis often drink too much, or take drugs or pills (sleeping pills, painkillers) to escape from thinking about their problems or in an attempt to soothe distress or some other unpleasant state of mind like frustration, depression or anxiety. Or they may try to treat some other problem, e.g. an inability to sleep or to relax, by using these substances.

Remember William whose case story we told you in the first chapter. As a businessman he had been used to taking clients out for meals, which involved a fair amount of alcohol. As his business began to fail he started drinking every night, often having three or four glasses of whisky to "unwind from the stresses of the day".

"As my difficulties increased and my whole business situation seemed more and more hopeless so the arguments at home between me and my wife increased. I found it more difficult to unwind and sleep without having drunk a large amount. It just helped to blot everything out. I would sit in front of the TV, drinking and smoking and often would finally drop off to sleep in my armchair. The more depressed I got the more I drank. What I didn't realize was that the drinking itself contributed to making me more depressed. It was a complete vicious cycle."

Like William, many people don't realize that alcohol, drugs and certain pills (tranquillizers, sleeping pills) can cause depression and anxiety or may make existing depression/anxiety worse. All these substances may remove inhibition and impair your judgement and therefore increase the likelihood of your responding to a crisis in a self-destructive way by hurting yourself.

SHOULD YOU BE WORRIED ABOUT YOUR ALCOHOL INTAKE?

What are the safe limits?

To calculate your weekly intake it is best to count up the units you drink:

1 unit of alcohol = half a pint of beer

= a single measure of spirits

= a glass of wine

= a small glass of sherry

= a measure of vermouth or aperitif

Drinks poured at home are usually much more generous than pub or restaurant measures. So, in calculating your units, you need to take this into account. Write down your daily intake in your diary for a week.

You may have read that for women up to 14 units a week and for men up to 21 units spread throughout the week, carries no long-term health risks. However, if you concentrate your drinking into, say, two bouts a week and get drunk, you are increasing the risks to yourself. If as a woman you drink more than 22 units per week or as a man more than 36 units a week, damage to your health is likely. Your liver and stomach can both be affected. Your concentration may be poor, and all sorts of personal and social problems may build up. There may be financial and legal problems, problems at work and home, and sexual difficulties, too.

Answer the following questions as honestly as possible[1]:

- Do you often drink too much, do you often think you should cut down? YES/NO
- Does alcohol cause problems for you and make you feel guilty? YES/NO
- Has anyone ever objected to your drinking or criticized you about it? YES/NO
- Have you ever had a drink in the morning to steady your nerves or to get rid of a hangover? YES/NO

---

[1] Adapted from Spitzer, R.L., Williams, J.B.W., Gibbon, M. and First, M.B. (1989). *Structured Clinical Interview for DSM-III-R*, SCIO, 9/1/89 Revision. New York: New York State Psychiatric Institute, Biometrics Research Department.

If the answer to one or several of these questions is YES, go on.

- Do you often find that, when you start drinking, you end up drinking more than you were planning to? YES/NO
- Do you often try to cut down or stop drinking alcohol? YES/NO
- Do you spend a lot of time drinking, being high or hung over? YES/NO
- Do you ever drink while doing something where it might be dangerous to drink at all (like driving)? YES/NO
- Do you drink so often that you start to drink instead of working or spending time at hobbies or with your family or friends? YES/NO
- Does your drinking cause problems with other people? YES/NO
- Does your drinking cause you significant psychological or physical problems? YES/NO
- Do you find you need to drink a lot more in order to get high than you did when you first started drinking? YES/NO
- Do you ever have the shakes when you cut down drinking? YES/NO

If you answered **more than three questions** with a definite **YES**, you are heading towards being dependent on alcohol. As long as you are taking alcohol it will be extremely difficult to make progress. You may want to contact your General Practitioner to see what services are available.

SHOULD YOU CUT DOWN OR STOP DRINKING?

If you decided from what you read above that you have problems with alcohol, you should cut down drinking or even avoid alcohol altogether. However, this may be hard to accept as alcohol, pills or drugs may have become like a trusted friend without whom you can't cope. Remember the exercises in Chapter 1 helping you to look at the pros and cons of self-harm and suicide? It may be useful to do a similar exercise regarding your drink. Try to think about what would be the advantages and disadvantages of continuing to drink and the advantages and disadvantages of giving up or cutting down. Think about advantages and disadvantages for yourself and for other people. Below we show you what Darren wrote (the young man whose story we told you about in Chapter 1). Darren thought that it would be too difficult for him to consider cutting down drinking, so he considered the advantages and disadvantages of continuing to drink versus those of stopping drinking altogether.

Advantages and disadvantages of continuing to drink

Advantages for myself	Disadvantages for myself
I like the taste of alcohol.	My girlfriend might leave me – she has told me several times how fed up she is with me being drunk – she says when I am drunk I am like a different person – much more aggressive.
It is good fun going to the pub with my mates and getting drunk.	
When I am a bit drunk I am a completely different person. I stop feeling bad about myself. I feel great, like anything is possible. I become much more sociable. I can talk to anybody.	I might get into serious trouble. Once or twice I've got into a fight when drunk. I could end up hurting someone seriously and then having to go to prison again. I might lose my driving licence.
It helps me forget some of the bad things that happened to me in the past.	

Advantages for others	Disadvantages for others
My friends like it when I go drinking with them. They all drink a lot too. I think seeing me make a fool of myself makes them feel less bad about their own drinking.	I did hit my girlfriend once when I was drunk. This might happen again. I could seriously hurt her.

Advantages and disadvantages of giving up drink

Advantages for myself	Disadvantages for myself
I wouldn't feel so hung over in the morning.	My mates wouldn't like me any more.
I have had to go in late to work on quite a few occasions because of that and have probably lost a couple of jobs because of it. I guess that wouldn't be so likely to happen if I stopped drinking.	It would be no fun being in the pub with them without drink.
I wouldn't end up like my mum who was an alcoholic. She died from liver problems, a slow and horrible death.	I'd miss that great buzz you get from the drink.

Advantages for others	Disadvantages for others
My girlfriend would be very pleased. She says I am much nicer when I am not drunk.	My friends would be put out.

When Darren thought about these advantages and disadvantages he decided that on balance he wanted to try to come off the drink as his relationship with his girlfriend mattered a lot to him.

Below you can fill in your own list of advantages and disadvantages. You may want to do this exercise twice and consider the pros and cons of cutting down versus those of stopping alcohol altogether.

Advantages and disadvantages of continuing to drink

Advantages for myself	Disadvantages for myself

Advantages for others	Disadvantages for others

Advantages and disadvantages of cutting down or giving up drink

Advantages for myself	Disadvantages for myself

Advantages for others	Disadvantages for others

What can you learn from this? What is your pattern? Are there more advantages or disadvantages of change? Which of the reasons for changing or not changing are the most important for you? If the reasons for not changing outweigh the reasons for change, what does that say? It may mean that you are very worried about losing a very valuable coping strategy. It may also mean that you are more addicted to alcohol than you had previously thought. Show your results to your doctor or therapist and discuss with them what help or support you might need to swing the balance in the direction of change.

HAVE THE GUTS TO STOP OR CUT DOWN DRINKING!

If you have decided that your alcohol intake is worrying and that you are ready to try to tackle this the following may be of help to you.

Many people tell us that all their friends drink and that their social life revolves round going to the pub and that it would be very difficult for them not to join in with their friends. However, not drinking is something that is becoming much more socially acceptable. Think of the parallel case of smoking. Five or ten years ago people who objected to others smoking in their presence were seen as weird, silly or wet and if they complained they had to endure sarcastic comments and abuse. Nowadays, with increased knowledge about the health risks of active and passive smoking, it is the smokers who are at the receiving end of the criticism.

Can you show some personal bravery if others bully you into drinking? "Oh come on, don't be a spoilsport, why don't you just have a tiny drink?" It can be very difficult to resist someone who is determined to get you to drink. But if your friends only accept you if you drink with them, are they really worth your while?

How to cut down

- Take small sips only. Count the number of sips it takes to finish a glass and then try increasing the number for the next glass and so on.

- Do something else enjoyable while drinking that will help distract attention from the glass – for example listening to music, talking, doing a crossword puzzle and so on.
- Instead of drinking your customary, favourite type of drink, change to something new. Changing the type of drink can help break old habits and reduce the amount drunk.
- Drink more slowly and concentrate on the flavour.
- Copy a slow drinker. Identify someone who drinks slowly and shadow them, not picking up the glass until they do.
- Put the glass down after each sip. If you hold the glass you will drink more often. Do something else with your hand instead of lifting the glass to the lips.
- Top up spirits with non-alcoholic drinks.
- As much as you can, buy your own drinks. If you have to go along with sharing rounds, do not buy yourself a drink when it is your round, or order a non-alcoholic drink.
- Take days of rest where you don't drink alcohol, at least one day per week, or preferably two, three or even four days per week. Take up other forms of entertainment or relaxation.
- Start drinking later than usual. For example, go to the pub later.
- Learn to refuse drinks. Role-play ways of saying no to drinks. Perhaps this is the most important assertiveness skill you need to learn. Say for example, "No thanks, I'm cutting down", or "I am not drinking tonight, I've got a bad stomach".

Stopping drinking altogether?

If after giving this careful consideration, you have decided to quit drinking rather than to cut down, you will need to consider the following points:

- You will definitely need to learn to refuse drinks and practise ways of saying "no".
- You will need to think about what are the situations in which you are most likely to want to reach for the bottle again and how are you going to deal with temptation?
- You may need to think carefully about re-structuring your social life, so that you do not just rely on going to the pub for meeting people.
- You may need to find other relaxing or fun activities.

You may find the problem-solving skills you learnt in Chapter 3 useful to brainstorm ideas for how to tackle the points above and to decide on a plan for how to put any changes into practice.

SHOULD YOU BE WORRIED ABOUT YOUR DRUG INTAKE?

This is a difficult question to answer in general, but perhaps the questions above in the alcohol section may help you to think about this. You may say: "What is wrong with having some ecstasy, cocaine or amphetamines amongst friends?" But are you really allowing yourself to think about the risks involved?

Look at the pros and cons of your drug use with your therapist.

SHOULD YOU BE WORRIED ABOUT YOUR CONSUMPTION OF TRANQUILLIZERS OR SLEEPING TABLETS?

This is again a difficult question to answer in general, as there are different reasons (some better, some worse) for why people are prescribed tranquillizers or sleeping tablets. Whilst on the whole it is not a good idea for people to be on tranquillizers or sleeping pills for a long time, now may not be the best time to come off them. Write down your reasons, if necessary with the help of your therapist.

If you do decide to come off your tranquillizers/sleeping tablets, it may be important to cut down gradually, rather than to risk severe withdrawal symptoms, especially if you have taken them regularly and for a long period of time. Discuss this with your therapist and your doctor. He/she may be able to help you devise a plan for cutting down. A useful self-help guide for cutting down/stopping tranquillizers/sleeping pills can be found in the book "*Bottling It Up*" by Curran and Golombok (for details see the reading list at the end of Chapter 6).

Even if you decide that it is too difficult to cut down or come off your tranquillizers/sleeping tablets at the moment, maybe you should consider regularizing your consumption. Rather than saying "on a bad day I allow myself up to five Lorazepam tablets, but on a good day I will only take one" a first step in the direction of gaining control over your tranquillizer habit might be to say "I will have three Lorazepam tablets a day only". That way you will avoid marked changes in your blood levels that could trigger off anxiety attacks.

HOW TO DEAL WITH SLEEPING DIFFICULTIES

If you have decided to come off alcohol, drugs, tranquillizers or sleeping tablets you may find it quite difficult to get to sleep at night. The following advice may help you to overcome this difficult period of time.

If you have difficulty going to sleep (from France, 1982)

* Do not drink endless cups of coffee or tea during the day. This will not help your sleep.
* Go to bed only when you feel really sleepy.
* Do not go to bed particularly early.

- Do not read, watch TV or eat in bed unless you are certain from your own past experience that these activities help you to get to sleep. When in bed try to get all your muscles as relaxed as you can.
- Do not think about getting to sleep or worry about the day's activities. Try instead to think about pleasant events or places.
- If you cannot find some pleasant thoughts at the moment, listen to sounds from outside the house – birds, people, traffic.
- If you are unable to fall asleep after 10 minutes get up immediately and do something else such as reading or going into a different room (if possible). Return to bed only when sleepy.
- Set your alarm and get up at the same time every morning irrespective of how much sleep you had during the night. Do not nap during the day.
- Once you are fully awake do not lie in bed worrying about not sleeping and daily problems but get up, go to a different room to make a drink if you feel like it and sit comfortably in a chair reading a book. It is often worthwhile to prepare a chair with a reading lamp and a rug if necessary and a suitable paperback the evening before.
- Only return to bed when you feel sleepy. When in bed relax thinking of pleasant events or places.
- If sleep does not come in 10 minutes, return to the chair and repeat the cycle.

KEY POINTS TO REMEMBER

- Drink and drugs whilst often providing some short-term relief do tend to make things more difficult in the longer term. They can cause depression and anxiety or make existing depression or anxiety worse.
- Drink and drugs make it easier to get into the frame of mind where you are likely to want to self-harm.
- It is important to try to understand what the positives/advantages of drinking or taking drugs are in your life. This is likely to give helpful clues towards what may be important needs in your life.
- Use your problem-solving skills (from Chapter 3) to help you think about how to deal with the challenges that cutting down or stopping drink/drugs will create in your life.

Advantages and disadvantages of continuing or cutting down drinking

Advantages and disadvantages of continuing to drink

Advantages for myself	Disadvantages for myself
Advantages for others	Disadvantages for others

Advantages and disadvantages of giving up drink

Advantages for myself	Disadvantages for myself
Advantages for others	**Disadvantages for others**

CHAPTER SIX

Some further thoughts

Maybe in drawing up the list of problems that are facing you now, you have realized that you cannot achieve the solutions you want without acquiring some new skills or digging out some old skills that you thought you no longer had.

Perhaps before you can move forward you have to deal systematically with a long-standing emotional issue that continues to preoccupy or undermine you. Discuss with your therapist how you can get further psychological help and also look at the reading list at the end of this chapter, which contains suggestions for further reading about specific problems, like relationship difficulties or lack of assertiveness.

For a long time to come the desire to harm yourself may be with you and with any crisis it may re-emerge.

Perhaps it is just a matter of not being too impatient with yourself and not having too high expectations of yourself. Give yourself time. Be on *your* side. Don't devalue your attempts to help yourself.

WHAT CAN YOU LEARN FROM THE PAST?

Try to think back to your attempt to harm yourself and look back over your description of the situation in Chapter 1. You may have managed to resolve the immediate situation that brought about your self-harm. It is worthwhile taking a note of this. It helps to remember that you have survived and what things are like for you now – how have you coped? What changes have you made? How does this make you feel now? You can look back on this when you find that life is difficult in the future and recall that you have coped in the past and felt better.

Try to answer the questions below in the space provided.

What do you think about your attempt at self-harm now?

With your new-found skills, what would you now do differently?

How do you feel now?

How can you prevent yourself from getting into a similar frame of mind?

If you have found it hard to feel better or to resolve the difficulties you were having when you self-harmed, you might like to think back to a time when you have coped and felt better. Remembering how you managed to cope in the past can be helpful. Please try to talk to your doctor or therapist if you are still having problems. It can take some time to feel better and more able to cope with problems.

Is your crisis plan still up to date?

Review this now, just in case you should once again feel like harming yourself. Who would you call? What strategies from Chapters 2, 3 or 4 would you use?

Don't just say: "It won't happen again". Give yourself time to think this through.

WHAT IF YOU FIND YOURSELF SLIPPING AGAIN?

Look over all the work you have done with the book. Is there anything that can help you out of the present dip? Re-read those sections that you found most helpful. Mark them in red. Continue to write a diary of moods and thoughts. You might also want to try some suggestions that Marsha Linehan, an American psychologist and a recognized expert in this area, has described to gain a sense of perspective (from Linehan, 1993). She has suggested some of the following ways of helping people through crisis.

Give yourself encouragement

Think positively. Repeat over and over: "I *can* stand it", "It *won't* last forever", "I will get over this. I am doing the best I can".

Focus on your long-term goals

Focus on your long-term goals and become more aware that your distress may be time limited and that it will not go on forever. If you have a good imagination, you might want to picture yourself several years from now. How would you like to picture your life? Where would you be? Who might be around you? What would you be doing? What would you be feeling? Try to have a positive picture in your mind, one that you would like to aim for. Try to have a picture that will bring you comfort at the moment and strength to carry on. You might also like to remember times when the emotional pain you have experienced in the past has ended and when life has been better.

"IF ONLY . . ." FROM CHANGE TO ACCEPTING WHAT CANNOT BE CHANGED

The most difficult aspect of coping with a distressing situation is to face up to the fact that some aspects of reality cannot be changed, no matter how hard you try.

Aileen's story

Aileen was a 23-year-old traffic warden who had come to the city from the North of Scotland. She felt she had escaped from a suffocating home environment to do her own thing. One year ago, Aileen developed severe asthma and as a result she had to spend many months in hospital, as despite intensive treatment her asthma wouldn't settle. As soon as she was out of hospital Aileen would start smoking again and only take her medication very haphazardly. When her doctor suggested that she should join a support group for asthma sufferers she got very angry. "I thought how dare she treat me like this. I could not accept that I was so ill. I felt like I was stuck in a nightmare from which I wanted to escape. Even my friends said I should take it easy for a bit but I just couldn't do it." In the end, Aileen got so frustrated and fed up with her problem that wouldn't go away that she took an overdose.

Dr Marsha Linehan wrote the following exercises to help people accept difficult aspects of reality.

Turning the mind

Acceptance of reality as it is, requires an act of choice. It is like coming to a fork in the road. You have to turn your mind towards the acceptance road and away from the "rejecting reality" road. You have to make an inner commitment to accept what cannot be changed. The commitment to accept does not itself equal acceptance. It just turns you toward the path. But it is the first step. You have to make the commitment over and over and over again. Sometimes you have to make the commitment many times in the space of a few minutes.

> Aileen found it very hard to accept that her asthma was serious and that it affected what she could do. To her it seemed that developing asthma was unjust and unfair. She felt very angry and frustrated. The thought of accepting her illness and its restrictions were at first unbearable for her. She had to deliberately begin to face the fact that she was ill before she could make any progress. She had to tell herself that she had to stop fighting against having asthma and get used to having to live *with* it.

Improve with meaning

This is about finding or creating some meaning or purpose in your pain. This involves focusing on whatever positive aspects of a painful situation you can find. This can help you to view your situation differently and allows that pain and distress to have a different function or meaning. This can help you to bear your pain.

> Aileen was only 23 when she became ill. She felt robbed of her youth and the fun she could have had, if only she had not developed asthma. Her friends told her later that they could not "get through" to her and that she had shut them out. She was uncomfortable when they expressed their concern for her and she often felt angry and misunderstood by her friends who seemed to want her to be more positive about her situation or when they seemed to be encouraging her to ignore her predicament. After some time, she began to realize that they were trying to understand how she felt and wanted to help her. Admittedly, their efforts sometimes backfired and Aileen felt even more isolated. However, she learnt to realize that they still valued her as a person and that having asthma did not affect this. Her friends had not written her off as being useless, as she had of herself. Having discovered this, she stopped viewing herself as someone with asthma who would not be able to lead the life she had planned for herself. She began to find that some areas of her life were less

affected by her illness than she had previously thought. She had major problems to solve such as not being able to continue as a traffic warden and having very little income. She could, however, still be a friend and an aunt – roles that she had valued before. Her suffering, and the impact it had on her life, had highlighted to her friends that their own health was precious and not to be taken for granted. She realized that she was more able to tune in to other people's distress and unhappiness and that she could be helpful to others. People found her easier to talk to, somehow less threatening, as she had experienced difficulties too. She heard from other people how others had coped in similar situations and how others admired them for either putting up with problems or finding ways round them. She had started on the path to accepting that her illness was likely to be permanent and that it did not need to affect all aspects of her life. She may have lost her good health but she had gained other things. Relationships were now more important to her than she had previously realized. She had not had a happy childhood but she could have a better adulthood and she still had opportunities open to her. Although her asthma was serious, she was still alive and that meant she still had options to make her life better than it had been before.

Like Aileen, all of us are aware that we do not have control over all aspects of our lives. We cannot turn the clock backwards and pretend that something has not happened, we cannot get back people we have lost through break-ups in relationships or through death, and we cannot always correct the mistakes in the past that we all make from time to time. These are the aspects of life that everyone finds hard to bear and that most of us cannot avoid. What we can do is try to find some meaning in our suffering.

FINAL WORDS: A NEW BEGINNING

We do not expect that having read this book everything will miraculously seem better, easier and more worthwhile to you. However, we do feel if you give yourself the chance to work through the exercises in the book and try to answer some of the questions and issues addressed as best and as truthfully as you can, that your chances of looking at things a bit differently, more broadly, more openly and perhaps more positively will have increased. Finding someone you can trust to help you is important. This could be someone you know, a friend or neighbour but we would also suggest you get help from your doctor. Your doctor can put you in touch with someone who is trained and experienced in helping help people who have self-harmed.

We hope that your life is now less painful to bear, and that you believe that you have options open to you. We wish you good luck now and in the future.

KEY POINTS TO REMEMBER

• Keep your crisis plan up-to-date.

If you find yourself slipping again:

• Revisit the skills learnt in earlier chapters.

Additionally:

• Give yourself encouragement.
• Focus on your long-term goals.
• Find or create some meaning or purpose in your pain.

Consider also whether you need some more intensive or long-term help.

FURTHER READING

Beating suicide

Ellis, T.E. and Newman, C.F. (1996). *Choosing to Live. How to Defeat Suicide Through Cognitive Therapy.* New Harbinger: Oakland, California.

Problem solving

Honey, P. (1983). *Solving Your Personal Problems.* Sheldon Press: London.
Prochaska, J.O., Norcross, J.C. and DiClemente, C.C. (1994). *Changing for Good: A Revolutionary Six-Stage Program for Overcoming Bad Habits and Moving Your Life Positively Forward.* Avon Books: New York.

Anger management

Hauck, P. *Calm Down: How to Cope with Frustration and Anger.* Sheldon Press: London.

Dealing with depression

Beck, A.T. (1976). *Cognitive Therapy and the Emotional Disorder.* Penguin Books: London.
Blackburn, I.M. (1994). *Coping with Depression.* Chambers: Edinburgh.
Burns, D.D. (1990). *The Feeling Good Handbook.* Plume: New York.
Greenberger, D. and Padesky, C.A. (1995). *Mind over Mood. A Cognitive Therapy Manual for Clients.* Guilford Press: New York.
Williams, C. (2001). *Overcoming Depression. A Five Areas Approach.* Arnold: London.

Self-esteem

Fennell, M. (1999). *Overcoming Low Self Esteem.* Robinson: London.
Palladino, C.D. (1989). *Developing Self-Esteem. A Positive Guide for Personal Success.* Kogan Page: London.

Wilde-McCormick, E. (1990). *Change for the Better. A Life-Changing Self-Help Psychotherapy Programme.* Unwin: London.

Assertiveness

Butler, P.E. (1982). *Self-Assertion for Women.* Harper and Row: New York.
Dickson, A. (1985). *A Woman in Your Own Right. Assertiveness and You.* Quartet Books: London.
Hare, B. (1988). *Be Assertive.* Macdonald Optima: London.

Relationship difficulties

Amodeo, J. and Wentworth, K. (1986). *A Guide to Successful Relationships.* Arkana: London.
Beck, A.T. (1988). *Love is Never Enough. How Couples Can Overcome Conflicts and Solve Relationship Problems Through Cognitive Therapy.* Penguin Books: London.
Norwood, R. (1986). *Women Who Love Too Much! When You Keep Wishing and Hoping He'll Change.* Arrow Books: London.
Skynner, R. and Cleese, J. (1983). *Families and How to Survive Them.* Methuen: London.

Childhood trauma and sexual abuse

Bain, O. and Saunders, M. (1990). *Out in the Open: A Guide for Young People Who Have Been Sexually Abused.* Virago: London.
Kennerly, H. (2000). *Overcoming Childhood Trauma.* Robinson: London.
Stones, R. (1987). *Too Close Encounters and What to Do About Them.* Magnet: London.

Drink and substance misuse

Curran, V. and Golombok, S. (1985). *Bottling It Up.* Faber and Faber: London.
Chick, J. and Chick, J. (1984). *Drinking Problems: Information and Advice for the Individual, Family and Friends.* Churchill Livingstone: Edinburgh.
Miller, W.R. and Munoz, R.F. (1983). *How to Control Your Drinking.* Sheldon Press: London.
Tyrer, P. (1986). *How to Stop Taking Tranquillizers.* Sheldon Press: London.

Other references

Bancroft, J., Hawton, K., Simkin, S., Kingston, B., Cumming, C. and Whitwell, D. (1979). The reasons people give for taking overdoses. *British Journal of Medical Psychology,* **52**, 353–365.
France, R. (1982). Help with sleeping problems. *Bulletin No. 8 of the International Committee for Prevention and Treatment of Depression.*
Linehan, M. (1993). *Skills Training Manual for Treating Borderline Personality Disorder.* Guilford Press: New York.
Williams, M. (1997). *The Cry of Pain. Understanding Suicide and Self-Harm.* Penguin Books: London.

What can you learn from the past?

What do you think about your attempt at self-harm now?

With your new-found skills, what would you now do differently?

How do you feel now?

How can you prevent yourself from getting into a similar frame of mind?

CHAPTER SEVEN

For relatives and friends

You may have been given permission to look at this book by the person you know who has harmed himself or herself. You may have just stumbled across this book and did not know that your friend or relative has harmed themselves. Either way it is likely that the fact that someone close to you has harmed herself or himself has a deep effect on you. It will probably have come as a shock to find this out.

You may feel upset, angry or confused about what has happened. You may think that others may blame you as having somehow contributed towards a situation that your relative or friend found too difficult to bear and tried to seriously harm themselves. You may have even thought that you are responsible and if only you had done or said something differently, this would not have happened.

Before you read on, we want you to know that you are not responsible for another person trying to harm themselves. When someone tries to harm themselves, they are unlikely to be thinking in a logical way and are likely to be viewing their problems as being overwhelming. Their resources to cope with their problems will have been greatly diminished and harming themselves may have seemed to be their only way out of an unbearable situation. Not only should you not blame yourself, you should also try not to be angry with them for having tried to harm themselves.

Most people once they have recovered from harming themselves realize that their friends and relatives do want to help them and may have noticed that something was wrong and that they were behaving out of character. Your relative or friend may have seemed to be depressed or overly sensitive or emotional to you in the recent past. It is likely that they have been struggling with their problems and have not been able to share the depth of their distress with anyone.

107

We know that when a person in such a state of distress is suicidal, they often think that they cannot ask for help, or accept help if it is offered. Often an individual will feel ashamed of being in such a deep state of distress or in a situation that they cannot readily resolve. They will often view their only way out of the situation as escape by self-harm. It is as if they have already closed off alternative options and ways to solve problems, and are only focusing on escape or a way out of intolerable distress. We know that you may be asking yourself why they did this or why they could not ask for help as you would have been more than willing to help, but in such deep distress they are unlikely to have viewed this as a realistic option.

Mark Williams, in his book *The Cry of Pain*, has described this as a catastrophic failure of empathy. He believes that suicidal despair switches off the ability to understand how others will react and feel. Although to you, the individual who has harmed himself or herself may appear to have disregarded the feelings of those close to him or her, it is likely that your friend or relative had little control over this and was unable to think through the potential consequence of self-harm for those to whom they are close.

WHAT CAN YOU DO NOW?

There may be no one right thing to say or right way to behave in this situation, but there are some things you can do to help both yourself and the person who has self-harmed.

YOUR OWN FEELINGS

The first thing you should do is to be aware of your own feelings about your relative or friend having harmed themselves. You may feel guilty, thinking that you have in some way contributed to the person close to you having harmed themselves. You may feel concerned and anxious that this will happen again and that you do not want to say or do something that may make the situation worse. You may feel shut out by the person who has self-harmed. It might be helpful to talk to someone you trust about your own feelings so that you can have some support for yourself in this situation. You may find that you are not alone in feeling the way you do as many people are affected by someone harming themselves. Often there are several people who have felt that they should be doing more to help someone who has been talking of harming themselves or behaving in a manner that suggests that they are distressed or troubled.

What if you have been implicated or blamed for the person self-harming? Clearly this would be a painful situation and you are likely to feel very distressed by this. You may feel angry. Try not to get drawn into the situation further and not to over-react. Trying to establish who is to blame, or who is being blamed is a pointless exercise. Try to move beyond this point. Again find someone who is open-minded to talk to before you talk to the person who has self-harmed. Most importantly, open up a dialogue with the person who has self-harmed. They are likely to have misunderstood your motives, feelings and behaviour. If you take a non-critical stance about why they have self-harmed and listen to what they have to say, then there is a reasonable chance that you will be able to clarify any misunderstandings that have arisen. What matters now is that they see you as someone who cares for them and who can help.

NON-CRITICAL LISTENING

Many people who self-harm are afraid that others would have criticized them for not being able to resolve their problems or for having resorted to harming themselves. It is important to listen to what the person has to say about their feelings and problems without being judgemental. As we have stated before, most people who try to harm themselves seriously have not been able to think clearly about the situation they are finding difficult and often feel too ashamed to talk to others about how they feel and think. By taking the person seriously and listening without criticizing, you can help a great deal to restore an individual's sense of self-worth and confidence in others.

INCREASING SELF-WORTH

After listening, there is more you can do. You can tell them that you value them and that they do matter to you and to others. Ask how you can help further but be prepared just to be there if you are needed and most importantly, keep communicating.

GETTING INVOLVED WITH LIFE AGAIN

We know that this may be a very emotionally draining time for everyone concerned. Talking and listening will help but it is also helpful to begin to do things together again. The individual who has harmed themselves may have been less active, more depressed and more withdrawn before they harmed themselves – as if they were disengaging from life. It will be helpful to involve them in activity again. Simple things such as going for a walk together, shopping, gardening or going out for coffee and cake can help to bring them in touch again with life.

PROFESSIONAL HELP

Lastly, after the crisis has passed and everything may appear back to normal, do not assume that it is. If someone has gone as far as to harm themselves seriously, the problems are unlikely to disappear completely in a short time. You can still keep communication between you open – talking and listening to them and helping them to get involved in things again. However, outside help may also be needed and you might want to encourage the individual to seek help through their doctor. In this way they will also have a professional person to help them.